Aaron and Jamie Ivey

EDITORIAL TEAM, LIFEWAY WOMEN PUBLISHING

Becky Loyd
Director, LifeWay Women

Tina Boesch
Manager, LifeWay Women Bible Studies

Sarah Doss
Editorial Project Leader, LifeWay Women Bible Studies

Mike Wakefield
Content Editor

Erin Franklin
Production Editor

Lauren Ervin
Art Director

Published by LifeWay Press® · © 2021 Aaron and Jamie Ivey

ISBN: 978-1-5359-9780-5

Item: 005822892

Dewey decimal classification: 306.81

Subject heading: MARRIAGE / HUSBANDS / WIVES

Unless otherwise noted, all Scripture quotations are taken from the ESV® Bible (The Holy Bible, English Standard Version®), copyright © 2001 by Crossway, a publishing ministry of Good News Publishers. Used by permission. All rights reserved. Scripture quotations marked (AMPCE) are taken from the Amplified Bible, Copyright © 1954, 1958, 1962, 1964, 1965, 1987 by The Lockman Foundation. Used by permission. Scripture marked BSB taken from The Holy Bible, Berean Study Bible, BSB Copyright © 2016, 2018 by Bible Hub. Used by Permission. All Rights Reserved. Scripture quotations marked (CEV) are from the Contemporary English Version. Copyright © 1991, 1992, 1995 by American Bible Society. Used by Permission. Scripture quotations marked (CSB) have been taken from the Christian Standard Bible®, Copyright © 2017 by Holman Bible Publishers. Used by permission. Christian Standard Bible® and CSB® are federally registered trademarks of Holman Bible Publishers. Scripture quotations from THE MESSAGE. Copyright © by Eugene H. Peterson 1993, 1994, 1995, 1996, 2000, 2001, 2002. Used by permission of NavPress. All rights reserved. Represented by TyndaleHouse Publishers, Inc. Scripture quotations marked (NIV) are taken from the Holy Bible, New International Version®, NIV®. Copyright © 1973, 1978, 1984, 2011 by Biblica, Inc.™ Used by permission of Zondervan. All rights reserved worldwide. www.zondervan.com. The "NIV" and "New International Version" are trademarks registered in the United States Patent and Trademark Office by Biblica, Inc.™ Scripture quotations marked (NLT) are taken from the Holy Bible, New Living Translation, copyright ©1996, 2004, 2007, 2013, 2015 by Tyndale House Foundation. Used by permission of Tyndale House Publishers, Inc., Carol Stream, IL 60188. All rights reserved.

Photo of the Iveys (p. 5) by Becca Matimba Photography, @bmatimbaphoto

Published in association with Jenni Burke of Illuminate Literary Agency: www.illuminateliterary.com

To order additional copies of this resource, write LifeWay Church Resources Customer Service; One LifeWay Plaza; Nashville, TN 37234; FAX order to 615.251.5933; call toll-free 800.458.2772; email orderentry@lifeway.com; or order online at www.lifeway.com.

Printed in the United States of America

LifeWay Women Publishing,
LifeWay Church Resources,
One LifeWay Plaza,
Nashville, TN 37234

table of contents

ABOUT THE AUTHORS

Aaron and Jamie Ivey live in Austin, Texas, where they parent four kids and do their best to change the world from right where they are. Jamie hosts the podcast, *The Happy Hour with Jamie Ivey,* has written some books, and will stop anything for some '90s hip-hop. Aaron is a pastor at The Austin Stone, has written some books, is a songwriter, and loves spending time cooking in the kitchen. They both believe that stories make a huge impact on the world and are honored to share their story and lives with others.

INTRODUCTION

We are so honored you would join us for this Bible study. We don't take it lightly that you'd show up, dive in, and do the diligent work of refining and cultivating a healthy marriage.

Throughout the two decades of our own marriage, we've been through sweet seasons and difficult times. We all know marriage isn't easy, and no one just stumbles into a healthy and vibrant marriage that overcomes hardship and stands the test of time. But we've found God faithful to give us strength, direction, and wisdom on how to endure and thrive through His Word.

As you do this study, we hope you are encouraged and challenged by stories from our own journey, but more than anything we want you to discover the surprising beauty of marriage by seeing God's heart and design for it. And the best place to see that is in Scripture. God is not silent about it, and He doesn't intend for you to build a meaningful marriage without His loving help. He's the One who invented it, so He's the One who is most passionate about seeing your marriage reflect His very heart.

We encourage you to engage with the content of the study alongside your spouse. We wrote this together with the hope you'd do it together. Set aside time every week to get into the Scripture, write your thoughts, and engage in meaningful conversation with your spouse on a planned date night.

We are on this journey with you. We are fighting for your marriage, even from a distance. You are not alone, and we hope and pray that God does a powerful work in your marriage.

Aaron & Jamie Ivey

HOW TO USE THIS STUDY

Welcome to *Complement*! We're so thankful you've chosen to do this study. We hope and pray you will truly see the beauty of marriage through Scripture in everything you read, study, view, and experience. To get started, we want to give you some information on how you can best use this study.

THE USER

Who is *Complement* for? While *Complement* was written and designed as a group Bible study for married couples, it is not limited to that type of use or that group of people. We also encourage engaged couples and almost-engaged couples to go through the study. It will certainly help lay a solid foundation for a godly, purposeful marriage. Also, regardless of whether you're a couple or an individual, you don't have to go through this with a group. The study is built in such a way that you can go through it on your own or maybe invite another couple to join you.

ELEMENTS OF THE STUDY

The study has two main parts: group time and personal study.

GROUP TIME

Once a week, you'll gather with your group to watch the teaching video. Aaron and Jamie will combine scriptural truth and personal experience to provide insight on different areas of marriage, including love, forgiveness, sex, mission, and more. Although the video teaching is included in the group time, the videos are also available for those who are going through the study individually. Go to *LifeWay.com/Complement* to purchase those videos. Your group time will also include review questions for the previous week's personal study and discussion prompts to help you debrief the video teaching.

PERSONAL STUDY

Between the group sessions, you will have three days of personal study to help you dig deeper into that session's subject. Those three days of study will include scriptural study and activity questions. As you work through each day, you'll note that we have designated a few questions as

"Connection Point" questions. These are questions we strongly encourage couples to talk through to help process what they are learning. The "Connection Point" questions will be identified with this icon:

Day 4 is called "Talk It Out." Here, we've provided a list of review questions to further help couples discuss and work through what they've learned during the three days of personal study.

The last section of the personal study is what we call "Date Night." Couples know how important it is to spend time together. But when we start talking about what to do, we either come up empty and do nothing, or we do the same "dinner and a movie" date over and over again. If that's you, we're here to help! Each week we'll provide you with two creative date ideas. We realize you may not like every idea, but our suggestions may spark other ideas you would enjoy. If you have great date night ideas, post them with the hashtag #ComplementStudy.

STUDY FLOW

To help you understand the order and flow of the study, here's what a sample week of the study might look like. For this example, we're going to say your group meets on Sunday night.

Sunday: Group meets for Session One. Possible agenda:

- Leader welcomes the group and initiates introductions.

- Start with some icebreakers and/or get-to-know-you questions.

- Play the Session One teaching video. Aaron and Jamie teach on the subject of "What Is Love?"

- Following the video, your group will debrief the teaching.

- Pray and dismiss.

Monday–Saturday: Complete the personal study for Session One.

- During the week you will work through Days 1–4 (which include "Talk It Out") of the personal study on "What Is Love?" Feel free to work through this material at your own pace.

- If possible, choose to do at least one of the "Date Night" ideas.

Sunday: Group meets for Session Two. Possible agenda:

- Leader welcomes the group.

- Use review questions to discuss what you learned in the Session One personal study.

- View the Session Two teaching video. Aaron and Jamie teach on "Placing Courage."

- Following the video, the group will debrief the teaching.

- Pray and dismiss.

This schedule continues in a consistent fashion until Session Seven. The agenda for the Session Seven Group Time will be the same as previous weeks. However, this video wraps up the study. No personal study will follow.

NOTE TO GROUP LEADERS

Check out the "Group Leader Tips" on pages 220–221 to help you lead your group more effectively.

WHAT IS LOVE?

T o love and be loved can mean a million different things to us. Whether we use love to describe how we feel about an evening walk under the canopy of starlight, a book we've read so many times the pages have worn thin, or the person we stood before in a crowd of witnesses and pledged our forevermore, we love, *love*.

GOD CREATED MARRIAGE TO ILLUSTRATE HIS UNBREAKABLE LOVE FOR US. MARRIAGE IS A METAPHOR OF JESUS' COVENANT RELATIONSHIP WITH THE CHURCH.

The entire Bible, from beginning to end, is one unified story. It is a story of a God-King who had so much love to give that He didn't want to keep it all to Himself. All of His work was good, but to Him, nothing was quite as special as His humans. He made every single person in His very own image. But these humans broke His heart by rejecting His love. Their rebellion invited a dark lord to master over the hearts of His beloved people. But God had a plan. He sent His only Son, Jesus Christ, to die a humiliating and painful death for the sins of His people. Jesus became sin so the people could become the righteousness of God (2 Cor. 5:21). This great exchange was, is, and always will be the most awesome demonstration of love.

This is love.

God created marriage to illustrate His unbreakable love for us. Marriage is a metaphor of Jesus' covenant relationship with the church. Pastor and author David Platt wrote:

> *When God made man, then woman, and then brought them together in a relationship called marriage, he wasn't simply rolling dice, drawing straws, or flipping a coin. He was painting a picture. His intent from the start was to illustrate his love for his people . . . For God created the marriage relationship to point to a greater reality. From the moment marriage was instituted, God aimed to give the world an illustration of the gospel.[1]*

Marriage is everything you imagine it to be—sometimes more and sometimes less. It's romance and partnership. It's a promise of *with*—someone to eat with, pay bills with, cry with, figure out how to do life with. It's someone to laugh with in the middle of the night at things no one else would find funny. It's having someone know you best, see you at your worst, and choose to love you still. Some days you will love your spouse to the moon and back, and others you won't feel an ounce of love for him/her. Marriage is for friendship, companionship, intimacy, and so much more. A good marriage has a myriad of benefits. None of those benefits or meanings are to be disparaged, but they are also not the ultimate purpose of marriage. So what is the ultimate purpose of marriage? In this study, we'll dive into the Scriptures to find out. We'll see just how purposeful and intentional God was in designing marriage, not just for our benefit, but for so much more.

NOTES

OPENING

1. Do you have a funny story surrounding your engagement or wedding? Please share it with the group.

2. What drew you to this study?

3. What is one way marriage is different than you thought it would be?

4. How does our current culture view marriage? How does that view support or oppose biblical marriage?

5. Name five characteristics of a good marriage and put them in order. Be ready to defend your choices.

WATCH THE VIDEO

DISCUSS

1. What part of the video really got your attention? Why?

2. Did you have a good model for the true meaning of love growing up? If so, explain. If not, how has that affected your ability to love others, especially your spouse?

3. How would you define *agape* love? Who do you know who loves people with that kind of love?

4. What hinders you from loving your spouse in that way?

5. How is marriage like a puzzle?

6. How are you and your spouse different? How do you love your spouse through the differences?

7. What have been some moments in your marriage when you had to "stay at the table" and work things out?

8. When you zoom out, how do you see God putting the pieces of your stories together in your marriage?

Teaching sessions available for purchase
or rent at *LifeWay.com/Complement*

A GREATER REALITY

Father,
Make me a person of love. Help me to be shaped and formed by Your love for me. Lead me to love others the way You have loved me.
Amen

MADE IN THE IMAGE OF LOVE

Marriage is a covenant of love between a man and woman. But for a husband and wife to experience a marriage that is unbreakable and full of love, we must first understand who we are as individuals. To do that, we must start at the very beginning.

Read Genesis 1:26-27.

What was God's purpose in creating humanity?

Every human being has been made in the likeness of God. This means we must look to God to know who we are and why we are here. We have to know who He is and what characteristics and desires He has shared with us.

Read 1 John 4:8 and write it below.

God is Love, Anyone who does not
Love others does not known God

In light of how this verse describes God, what does He share with us?

✳ Being made in the image of God also means[we are made in the image of love.]Love is in our DNA, our souls, our very beings. We are born with a desire to love and be loved. Your desire and need for love is not wrong or too big. You were created to be loved fully and completely.

Do you ever feel silly, needy, or ashamed by how deeply you want to be loved? If so, explain what makes you feel that way.

How does[Genesis 1:27]encourage you to not minimize or belittle your desire to be loved?

So God created humans to be like Himself.

In his book *The Weight of Glory*, C. S. Lewis said it this way:

> *. . . it would seem that Our Lord finds our desires not too strong, but too weak. We are half-hearted creatures, fooling about with drink and sex and ambition when infinite joy is offered us, like an ignorant child who wants to go on making mud pies in a slum because he cannot imagine what is meant by the offer of a holiday at the sea. We are far too easily pleased.[2]*

In what ways have you made "mud pies" instead of receiving God's "offer of a holiday at the sea"? What keeps you from being insatiably discontent with the lesser offerings of the world? How would your life change if you were?

WHAT IS THE PURPOSE OF MARRIAGE?

God created us [to be in relationship with] Him, represent Him to everyone around us, and use all of the intelligence, creativity, and abilities He has given us to cause the world to flourish. Isn't that incredible? In the beginning of creation, God used a garden to teach us this concept. God called Adam to work the garden of Eden. But as Adam was digging and planting and taking care of the animals, God noticed something Adam couldn't see for himself.

Read Genesis 2:15-18.

What did God see that Adam needed that Adam did not realize or see on his own?

*The Hebrew word for **helper** ('ezer) means, "one who supplies strength in the area that is lacking in the 'helped.' The term does not imply that the helper is either stronger or weaker than the one helped."[3]*

Man alone was insufficient to represent God to the world. God's creation of humanity was only half-finished. So God [made for man a partner, a friend, a helper—a person like him but not like him.] Men and women are equal image bearers of God, but they are [also distinct from each other.] Those distinctions are necessary for the world to see a full representation of God. And both men and women are necessary to move the human project forward to flourishing.[4]

In our current culture, the word *helper* has gotten a bad rap. It is often implied that a *helper* is less than or a person of less dignity. We think of a *helper* in terms of a Robin to a Batman—Batman is necessary; Robin is not. But this is completely wrong. God made woman because man could not fulfill God's calling alone. Men need women, and women need men. However culture may slice it and divvy out importance, weight, and significance, God says for the world to see a true picture of Him and for the world to move forward in peace and flourishing, we *equally* need men and women.

Imago Dei is Latin for "**the image of God.**" Every person is created in the image of God, which implies that an intrinsic value, beauty, and worth is found in every single human being.[5]

Misunderstanding the *imago Dei* is often what causes confusion and turmoil in marriages.

How might a misunderstanding of the value of men and women damage a marriage? In what ways have you seen your life flourish through partnership with your spouse?

MORE   SATISFIED
"   whole
"   happy
NOT   ashamed

Genesis 2:24-25 gives us a peek into the very first marriage.

Therefore a man shall leave his father
and his mother and hold fast to his wife,
and they shall become one flesh.
And the man and his wife were both
naked and were not ashamed.

In the Scripture above, circle what God intends for a husband and wife to experience within a covenant relationship.

So, if God's ideal marriage was the joining of Adam and Eve, what went wrong? Let's take a look at Genesis 3:1-13.

CONNECTION POINT

Discuss your answers to these questions together.

Focus on verses 1-5. How did Satan lie and deceive Eve? How has this kind of lying and deception caused turmoil and distrust in your relationship with God? In your marriage?

CREATED DOUBT

How was Adam and Eve's relationship with God changed as the result of their sin (v. 8)?

SINS DISTORTS

Conscience — Sensitive to θ
hid from θ

In Genesis 3:7,10,12, how was Adam and Eve's relationship with one another changed as the result of their sin, specifically in regards to "one flesh" (Gen. 2:24) and "naked" and "not ashamed" (v. 25)?

Knew They were
Naked
Now ashamed

Although Adam and Eve sinned, which distorted their relationship with each other and with God, God still had a perfect plan. Jesus became the Redeemer for our salvation and the perfect example of an unending, unchanging, unbreakable love. And now, despite the fall, one of God's most profound and powerful ways of demonstrating His love to the world is through His design of covenantal marriage. See, when God designed marriage, He intended it to reflect the eternal covenant between Christ and the church. Isn't that amazing? It's a living, breathing illustration of the covenant He's made with us! But it's not a perfect example because we're not perfect. At times, sin distorts the reflection, making it impossible for us to clearly see God's love for us, much less display it to the world. That's why our primary focus is on Jesus to show us the way of love. He is our perfect example—our glasses, if you will—enabling us to see God and to love God. He transforms us by His love to be people who love.

Read Ephesians 5:22-33 (emphasis added).

> *Wives, submit to your own husbands, as to the Lord. For the husband is the head of the wife even as Christ is the head of the church, his body, and is himself its Savior. Now as the church submits to Christ, so also wives should submit in everything to their husbands.*

> *Husbands, love your wives, as Christ loved the church and gave himself up for her, that he might sanctify her, having cleansed her by the washing of water with the word, so that he might present the church to himself in splendor, without spot or wrinkle or any such thing, that she might be holy and without blemish. In the same way husbands should love their wives as their own bodies. He who loves his wife loves himself. For no one ever hated his own flesh, but nourishes and cherishes it, just as Christ does the church, because we are members of his body. "Therefore a man shall leave his father and mother and hold fast to his wife, and the two shall become one flesh." This mystery is profound, and I am saying that it refers to Christ and the church. However, let each one of you love his wife as himself, and let the wife see that she respects her husband.*

Need to submit to Xr

Read all of the highlighted verses. What does the word *as* show you about the greater meaning of marriage?

It's a Mystery
Need Xr's help

Write down everything listed in those verses that Christ does
for the church. *Xt is the Head, loves the ch died for the ch etc. Submission sanctify Forgives*

Take a moment to consider some ways that your marriage
reflects the glorious kindness of Christ and the church.

*Forgiving
does not hold on to wrongs done
Submitting to one another*

Through this Scripture, we see that God not only commands us to treat our
spouses in a certain way, He also gives us tangible examples of what that
looks like through the relationship of Christ and the church. Do you see how
high the standard is for husbands and wives—and their love for each other?

**Ephesians 5:1-2,21 gives us the framework for these
instructions on how a husband and wife should treat one
another. Read it below.**

> *Therefore be imitators of God, as beloved children.
> And walk in love, as Christ loved us and gave himself
> up for us, a fragrant offering and sacrifice to God.
> . . . submitting to one another out of reverence
> for Christ.*

According to these verses, what are the most important things
we should remember and do as we walk out our marital roles?

Need to Remember why we got married

<u>Marriage is hard</u>. A million things can cause us to forget why we chose one another in the first place—<u>work</u>, <u>kids</u>, <u>money</u>, <u>sex</u>, and on and on. We need to be reminded a million times over why we got married and what God purposed for our marriage.

Southern California's Highway One stretches across some of the nation's most beautiful landscapes. For six hundred fifty miles you can weave in and out of the Redwoods, up and down the mountains, and around and around the most fragrant bends of prairie and ocean. It's not a quick drive, but you can experience the breathtaking coast of California by stopping at one of the many vistas.

When you're tucked into the height of the redwoods or a curve of the road that sends you far to the east, the ocean feels forever away—kind of forgotten. That doesn't mean the ocean has disappeared, but it's just more difficult to see from your vantage point. Similarly, we can get lost in the complexities and difficulties of marriage and lose sight of the purpose. But going to Scripture calls us back to the ultimate aim of our marriage. It's like finding our way to one of those vistas where we can see the ocean clearly again. The Bible helps us remember what marriage is all about and how to make the necessary adjustments to get back on track.

In Scripture, from the first marriage in the garden of Eden to the marriage feast of the Lamb, God has used the theme of marriage to reflect His relationship with His people. His <u>covenant love</u> and <u>faithfulness</u> set the standard for how we are to love our spouses. In marriage, when we say, "I do," we are making a similar covenant with our spouse.

We promised "I do"
Remember your vows

What similarities do you see in the passages about God's covenant love for His people on the left to the sample marriage vows on the right?

SCRIPTURE	MARRIAGE VOWS
Know therefore that the LORD your God is God, the faithful God who keeps covenant and steadfast love with those who love him and keep his commandments, to a thousand generations (Deut. 7:9).	*I dedicate this marriage today and this home tomorrow to the Lordship of Jesus Christ. I will never leave you or forsake you. Wherever you go, I will go. Where you live, I will live; Where you die,*
"For the mountains may depart and the hills be removed, but my steadfast love shall not depart from you, and my covenant of peace shall not be removed," says the LORD, who has compassion on you (Isa. 54:10).	*I will die; Your people will be my people, and your God my God; May the Lord bring anguish upon me if anything but death separates us. I give all of myself to you.*
The LORD your God is in your midst, a mighty one who will save; he will rejoice over you with gladness; he will quiet you by his love; he will exult over you with loud singing (Zeph. 3:17).	with us always "in our mi. dst" happy for us ① will calm us " " Rejoice over us
And I will betroth you to me forever. I will betroth you to me in righteousness and in justice, in steadfast love and in mercy. I will betroth you to me in faithfulness. And you shall know the LORD (Hos. 2:19-20).	*I take you to be my wife/husband, to have and to hold from this day forward, for better, for worse, for richer, for poorer, in sickness and in health, to love and to cherish, till death do us part.*
"Therefore a man shall leave his father and mother and hold fast to his wife, and the two shall become one flesh." This mystery is profound, and I am saying that it refers to Christ and the church (Eph. 5:31-32).	cleave to write 2 are 1

A profound sense of joy, sacrifice, grace, and permanence is reflected in God's unconditional love for us. The same should be at the heart of our love and marriages so that we might reflect Him to the world.

Are we going to always get this perfect? No. Marriage is never a straight shot to bliss. We love; we fight; we make up; we mess up—over and over and over and over again. But how does remembering God's purpose for marriage help you reset when things get difficult in marriage? How does it stir in you a desire to never give up on what God has called you to in marriage?

AS YOU GO

Remember this truth: "And I will betroth you to me forever. I will betroth you to me in righteousness and in justice, in steadfast love and in mercy. I will betroth you to me in faithfulness. And you shall know the LORD" (Hos. 2:19-20).

(handwritten) God's unbreakable Love

Fight for this truth: God created marriage to illustrate His unbreakable love for you. You are made to be loved and to love. Your desire to be loved is not too big, too annoying, or too needy. But the world's offer of love will never satisfy our deep need for love; only God's love will satisfy.

Pray this truth: *God, thank You for Your Word. Thank You for teaching me . . .*

Help me to trust and obey You with . . .

Amen

DAY

GOD'S
BELOVED

Father,
I ask that You use Your Word to teach me
about Yourself. Renew my mind to think
about love the way You think about love.
Transform my heart through the sacrificial
love of Jesus Christ. Help me to love You,
love my spouse, and love my neighbors with
the kind of love with which You love me.
Amen

Our definition of *love* is formed by our relationships and experiences. For many of us, this often creates a chasm of dissonance between what we hope to experience and what we have actually experienced.

Think about it like this. We are told, "God loves you." But we understand this declaration of love through our experiences of love. This is how it might translate: *God loves you. God [is going to say He loves you, but then He's going to get tired of you messing up all the time and leave] you. God loves you. God [says beautiful things but does the opposite of that thing] you. God loves you. God [cares most about your happiness and will never ask you to do something hard] you.*

This language disconnect makes it crucial that we define our terms according to the standard of truth. Because we believe God is the essence of love, we believe we have no better Source from whom to derive our definition, belief, and expression of love. Our hope is that as we grow in knowledge of God's love for us, our love for Him and one another will be awakened.

Write out what love means to you on the next page.

If I'm totally honest, love has meant this to me . . .

_____

_____

_____

_____

_____

No doubt your response has been shaped by family, experiences, education, and culture. If we had parents who fed, clothed, and cared for us, we may have developed a sense that love is security. If we had a cinematic meet-cute, we may believe romantic love is a spontaneous gift of magic from the universe. If we have experienced betrayal, death, or abuse in relationships with people we loved, we might have very little faith in "love."

Using the word bank below, jot down in the spaces provided how the following people or experiences have impacted your experience with love.

inspiring	sex	magical	just a word
disappointing	loyalty	vulnerable	commitment
selflessness	short-lived	friendship	happiness
passion	trust	acceptance	betrayal
unconditional	conditional	compassion	feeling at home with a person

Family (parents, siblings, close relatives, etc.)

Friends

Faith

Culture (art, literature, music, social media, geographic
locations, etc.)

Impactful Experiences (both positive and negative)

Understanding love can be extremely difficult because our view of love is so often shaped and defined by broken and sinful humans. People will always fall short in their ability to love perfectly, but God will not. God's love is pure. It is blameless. It is without fault. To truly understand love, we need to look at the One who loved us first. It's when we see His love that we'll begin to understand how much better and altogether different His definition of *love* truly is.

Read the following passages and highlight or circle the word *love* every time it's used:

This is my commandment, that you love one another as I have loved you. Greater love has no one than this, that someone lay down his life for his friends.
JOHN 15:12-13

This is how we know what love is: Jesus Christ laid down his life for us. And we ought to lay down our lives for our brothers and sisters.
1 JOHN 3:16, NIV

Dear friends, let us love one another, because love is from God, and everyone who loves has been born of God and knows God. The one who does not love does not know God, because God is love. God's love was revealed among us in this way: God sent his one and only Son into the world so that we might live through him. Love consists in this: not that we loved God, but that he loved us and sent his Son to be the atoning sacrifice for our sins. Dear friends, if God loved us in this way, we also must love one another.
1 JOHN 4:7-11, CSB

What is the importance of understanding we were loved by
God first?

How do these passages say Jesus demonstrated God's love
for us?

How does God call us to demonstrate our love for one
another?

Our ability to love God and one another is not dependent on our personal
experience with love, our personality type, or our willpower. True, genuine,
transformative love is not that we have loved God, but that He has loved
us. This is where all of love begins—receiving the impeccable, all-satisfying,
never-ending love of God. Scripture shows us this love was best displayed
for us through the atoning sacrifice of His Son, Jesus Christ.

Sacrifice is a daunting, unpopular concept. Our western culture promotes
a lifestyle of having everything we think we deserve, when we want it
and how we want it. We don't like the idea of sacrificing anything. Our
consumer-driven society reveals how little we actually value any type of real
sacrifice. When we do hear stories or quips about sacrifice, it's generally in
terms of a player or soldier "taking one for the team." This is what Paul
was talking about in Romans 5:6-7.

> *For while we were still weak, at the right time Christ*
> *died for the ungodly. For one will scarcely die for*
> *a righteous person—though perhaps for a good person*
> *one would dare even to die.*

Maybe, just maybe, we would sacrifice our lives for a really good person, a person we love, a person we're devoted to, a friend.

But that's not what we see Jesus did.

Read Romans 5:8-10.

> ... but God shows his love for us in that while we were still sinners, Christ died for us. Since, therefore, we have now been justified by his blood, much more shall we be saved by him from the wrath of God. For if while we were enemies we were reconciled to God by the death of his Son, much more, now that we are reconciled, shall we be saved by his life.

Underline every description of who Jesus Christ died for. What do you learn about who Jesus died for?

Fleming Rutledge wrote,

> If we think of Jesus' sacrifice in the same way that we think of soldiers in wartime, therefore, we will miss the entire point. Jesus is speaking to a group of people who are not going to be beside him on the battlefield. Quite the opposite. They have consistently misunderstood him and are about to deny and abandon him. The twelve disciples are very poor excuses for friends. Only in the sacrifice of Jesus are they transformed from enemies into friends.[6]

Sacrifice is a romantic ideal. It's an exquisite demonstration and manifestation of love. And most of us, if placed in a do-or-die situation, would lay our lives down for our spouses. Where marital sacrifice gets difficult is in the everyday, ordinary practice of self-sacrifice for the sake of love and unity. And the longer we are married, the more we are tempted to stop sacrificing. We become dull in our awareness of needing to sacrifice for our spouses.

CONNECTION POINT

Discuss your thoughts on this exercise together.

Read the following scenarios. What do you think it could look like to walk in sacrificial love in each of these circumstances?

1. You come in from a long day at work, and you can see it all over her face—stress, anxiety, weariness. She's done. But so are you. It might not have been a two-year-old pulling at you all day, but adult coworkers aren't any easier. All you want is to take a half hour of some quiet time.
2. For days he has been in a funk. Moody. Short. It feels like he hasn't seen you at all. You feel utterly disregarded.
3. She asks without looking up, "Would you mind grabbing me another cup of coffee?" You didn't intend to, but a scorecard appeared in your head, and you checked off another box of when you got her coffee. And seeing all the checks—picking up dry cleaning, giving the kids a bath, dropping a load of clothes in-between client calls, mowing the yard, running the kids all over tarnation—sends you spiraling.
4. He never wants to have sex. You wonder how long it will take for him to initiate if you don't.

It's possible these illustrations brought a recent situation to mind in which you didn't love your spouse as sacrificially as you wish you would have. If God is bringing a moment to mind, spend some time praying and repenting. Reflect on how Jesus' sacrificial love inspires and compels you to love your spouse.

We are called to present our bodies as a living sacrifice before God. Paul wrote:

> *I appeal to you therefore, brothers, by the mercies of God, to present your bodies as a living sacrifice, holy and acceptable to God, which is your spiritual worship.*
> **ROMANS 12:1**

Underline the phrase "by the mercies of God." The NIV translation of the phrase is—"in view of God's mercy." Read the verse again, this time substituting "by the mercies of God" with "in view of God's mercy."

> *in view of God's mercy*
> *I appeal to you therefore, brothers, ~~by the mercies of God~~, to present your bodies as a living sacrifice, holy and acceptable to God, which is your spiritual worship.*
> **ROMANS 12:1**

How does the phrase "in view of God's mercy" motivate you to live a life of sacrifice?

How can you consistently keep this phrase in mind?

Read Hosea 6:6 and write it below.

Eugene Peterson paraphrased the verse like this, "I'm after love that lasts, not more religion. I want you to know GOD, not go to more prayer meetings" (Hos. 6:6, The Message).

In what ways have you put religion above love in your relationship with God?

In what ways have you made cold, "take-one-for-the-team" sacrifices in marriage without considering God's mercy in His sacrifice for us?

 *AS YOU GO*

Remember this truth: "This is my commandment, that you love one another as I have loved you. Greater love has no one than this, that someone lay down his life for his friends" (John 15:12-13).

Fight for this truth: Your ability to love is not dependent on what your past or present experience with love is, how loving your personality is, or what kind of day you are having. Your ability to love is rooted in God's transformative love for you.

True, genuine, transformative love is not that we have loved God but that He has loved us. This is where all of love begins—receiving the impeccable, all-satisfying, never-ending love of God.

Pray this truth: *God, thank You for Your Word. Thank You for teaching me . . .*

Help me to trust and obey You with . . .

Amen

DAY 3

A LOVE LIKE NO OTHER

Father,
No love could ever compare to Yours.
Teach me to love my spouse in a way that
reflects Your perfect love. I am incapable
of loving perfectly, but with the help of
Your Holy Spirit, empower me to love in
a way that helps my spouse see Jesus. As
I sit in Your Word today, my heart is open
to receive what You have to say.
Amen

Today, we will study the passage that has been read at weddings worldwide—1 Corinthians 13, affectionately known as the love chapter. Although it wasn't originally written in the context of marriage, there's a good reason it's read at so many covenant ceremonies. It's beautiful, lofty, and empowering. Every lovestruck couple truly believes they will be the ones who embody every phrase and finally get marriage right.

However, we must keep in mind why Paul wrote this beautiful charge to love one another so vigorously and relentlessly. The church at Corinth was in grave trouble. She was fractured because of the people's pride, self-importance, and power. Their disunity was distracting them from advancing the gospel. Paul told them what they needed to hear to correct the problems, heal the body, and function in unity again.

Remembering God's love for us and His command to love others as He loved us is the antidote to heal the brokenness in our hearts and marriages that comes from pride, self-importance, wounds, and distance.

The love chapter teaches the preeminence, perfection, and permanence of love.

THE PREEMINENCE OF LOVE

Read 1 Corinthians 13:1-3 and write it below.

Draw a box around the phrase "but have not love" or "do not have love" (CSB) every time it's used. What did Paul say is worthless without love?

Paul wrote about a love that is preeminent, or superior, to all other things. He said love is so supreme that if he didn't have love, he *was* nothing (v. 2) and he *gained* nothing (v. 3).

What do you think he wanted us to understand and believe by writing these two statements?

Paul stated that having the ability to speak well, to speak with the gift of tongues, to have prophetic powers, and spiritual wisdom, all faith, generosity, and a heart of sacrifice—all amazing things—are less than the importance of having love.

Out of the gifts and abilities listed, which ones seem the most important to you? Why do you think love might seem less effective than these other traits or gifts?

THE PERFECTION OF LOVE

Read 1 Corinthians 13:4-8a.

What an incredible description of love. Sometimes, this type of love may seem unattainable, but the hope found in Scripture is that God actually wants to teach, empower, and develop this kind of love within each of us. One of the best ways to grow in love for each other is to take the time to examine how you're currently doing in loving each other. Take an honest inventory of how you want to grow and how your spouse is growing. Then, remind yourself how Jesus perfectly expresses this love toward you.

LOVE	Definition	How have you seen Jesus perfectly express this aspect of love?	What is an example of how your spouse has expressed this aspect of love to you?	In what way do you want to grow in expressing this aspect of love to your spouse?
Is Patient	*to not lose heart; to be long-suffering in bearing the offenses and injuries of others*			
Is Kind	*of good and benevolent nature or disposition; considerate*			
Does Not Envy	*covet; to be discontent with regard to another's advantages*			
Does Not Boast	*to speak with excessive pride, especially about oneself*			

Is Not Arrogant	*claims to superior importance or rights; overbearingly assuming*			
Is Not Rude	*impolite in a deliberate way*			
Does Not Insist On Its Own Way	*demanding our preferences or rights*			
Is Not Irritable	*easily excited to impatience or anger*			
Is Not Resentful	*to feel or show displeasure or indignation from a sense of injury or insult*			
Does Not Rejoice At Wrong-doing	*to feel happy when someone else commits a blame-worthy action or behavior*			
Rejoices With the Truth	*celebrates when someone acts or behaves in correspon-dence with the Word of Truth*			

CONNECTION POINT

Discuss your answer to this exercise together.

Choose one or two of the characteristics of love and share with your spouse how well he/she has expressed this aspect of love to you. Encourage your spouse in the ways you see God loving you through him/her.

....

....

....

....

Read 1 Corinthians 13:7 from your Bible. Then, read it again from the AMPC:

> *Love bears up under anything and everything that comes, is ever ready to believe the best of every person, its hopes are fadeless under all circumstances, and it endures everything without weakening.*
>
> **1 CORINTHIANS 13:7**

This is an undeniably high bar for love. Most of us desire to love one another this fully and completely but have subconscious (or conscious) limits.

Being as honest as possible, what limits your love? Describe the circumstance that could cause you to quickly believe the worst about your spouse or could cause the love and hope in your marriage to fade.

THE PERMANENCE OF LOVE

Read 1 Corinthians 13:8b-13.

How did Paul stress the permanence of love in this passage?

Paul wrapped up this section by showing that everything passes away—
nothing is permanent in this world. Even the spiritual gifts the Corinthians
put so much stock in—prophecy, tongues, and knowledge—were going
to cease. Everything we are able to see, however clear it might seem to us
in the moment, is merely a shadow or a portion. What will remain? Faith,
hope, and love, with the greatest being love. Love never fails (1 Cor. 13).
Why not? Perhaps because love is the "essence of God's character."[7] The
greatest love of our life is merely an imitation of the supremacy, perfection,
and permanence of the love of Jesus Christ.

Read Deuteronomy 31:6.

What did God promise Joshua?

What did He say Joshua would experience if he trusted this
promise?

Permanence breeds an environment for trust, love, security, vulnerability,
and intimacy. We have no control over when death may part us from our
spouse, but we are called to imitate Christ in the permanence of love.
Dr. Timothy Keller wrote, "Real love, the Bible says, instinctively desires
permanence."[8]

CONNECTION POINT

Discuss your answers to these questions together.

Spend a few minutes assessing your marital environment. Is there any fear, anxiety, or dread present because of the thought that your love for one another may not be permanent?

....

....

....

....

What would it look like to renew strength and courage in your relationship through the reminder that you're not going anywhere? Discuss with your spouse.

....

....

....

....

AS YOU GO

Remember this truth: "Love bears up under anything and everything that comes, is ever ready to believe the best of every person, its hopes are fadeless under all circumstances, and it endures everything without weakening" (1 Cor. 13:7, AMPC).

Fight for this truth: No one can and will love you as fully, deeply, and faithfully as God will. The more we surrender to the love of God and the more we depend on the Holy Spirit to help us love, the more we will be able to show our spouses the kind of love we so desperately want to and need to.

Pray this truth: *God, thank You for Your Word. Thank You for teaching me . . .*

Help me to trust and obey You with . . .

Amen

TALK
IT OUT

We encourage you to take a few minutes on this day to sit with your spouse and process what you studied this week. Use some or all of the following questions to guide your discussion:

1. Which day of study was your favorite and why?

2. What was the most difficult portion of the study for you and why?

3. Do you think we truly understand the purpose of marriage? Why or why not?

4. How well does our marriage reflect the gospel and the love of Christ?

5. How has our understanding of love shaped our marriage for better or worse?

6. How do we display sacrificial love for each other? How can we get better at that?

7. Which of the characteristics of love from 1 Corinthians 13 do you struggle with the most?

8. How can we help each other in the areas of love we're weakest in?

9. Which of the "As You Go" statements really captured your heart? Why?

Finish this day by praying together. Express your gratefulness for the love Christ has shown and also given you to express to each other. Spend some time praying about the areas of your marriage that God has revealed to you that need attention or refining.

It's so important that you and your spouse spend quality time together on a consistent basis. You'll need to be purposeful and intentional to make this happen. We want to help. Each week we'll provide one or two simple date night ideas. Of course, "date night" could be a "date morning" or "date afternoon." Whatever best fits your schedule. And if you're wondering what to talk about, feel free to use the designated connection points found throughout this week's study or the discussion questions found on Day 4.

DATE IDEAS FOR THIS WEEK

1. Make a picnic meal and head to a local park. The meal can be as simple or elaborate as you want it to be. Find a picnic table or just throw an old quilt down under a shade tree and enjoy time with each other.

2. Grab a puzzle out of the closet or go purchase a new one. Open the box, dump out the pieces, and work together on it. (Just don't work in silence!) Have some great conversation as you work.

PLACING

COURAGE

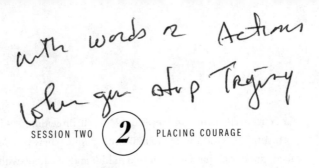

with words or Actions
when you stop Trying

*Y*ou got this. I believe in you. I'm
in this with you. These types of
phrases fuel our courage. These
encouraging words take us from
a fear-filled "I could never do that!" to
a courageous "I'm going for it!"

> *JUST AS I WAS WITH*
> *MOSES, SO I WILL BE*
> *WITH YOU. I WILL*
> *NOT LEAVE YOU OR*
> *FORSAKE YOU.*
> *JOSHUA 1:5b*

God spoke similar words to encourage Joshua
to accept the arduous and terrifying task of leading God's people to their
inheritance. Joshua had every reason to be terrified. He was about to step
into Moses' shoes and lead a giant group of grumbling, disobedient, cranky
people into the land that God had promised them. He must have been
scared out of his wits and sad that he even had to take this role. Surely his
heart was grieving, missing his friend and leader.

When God addressed Joshua, God didn't ignore Joshua's fear or sadness.
Instead, God made an incredible promise to him: "Every place that the
sole of your foot will tread upon I have given to you, just as I promised to
Moses" (Josh. 1:3). It's a lot like revealing the end of a mystery novel to
someone—don't worry, we already know what happens, and you win.

Then God said to Joshua—don't be afraid, I've got your back. Or in
God's words, "Just as I was with Moses, so I will be with you. I will
not leave you or forsake you" (Josh. 1:5b). Just in case Joshua needed

praying always prayer about me
to other my biggest
Affirmations fan

47

extra encouragement, God repeated Himself three times—"Be strong" (Josh. 1:6-7,9). God wanted to make sure Joshua knew he could do all God called him to do, that God believed in him and would be with him the entire time.

Story after story in Scripture shows us God is not only fully aware of the hardship we face but is in our corner cheering the loudest. He promises He will be with us in every dark valley, every painful step. He will bring us through. God doesn't command us to do the hard thing and then stand back and watch to see if we can. No, He enters in. He comes close. So close, in fact, that He chooses to dwell in the hearts of His saints.

Encouraging someone means putting courage in that person. We need courage to face difficulty, to do hard things, to endure when we feel weary and weak. It seems God made us to be motivated and inspired through His help and the help of our community. We go to His Word to be reminded of who He is, who we are in Him, and what He has called us to do. His Word encourages us to grow in faith, wisdom, discernment, and courage to step out in that calling.

Brennan Manning wrote, "Lodged in your heart is the power to walk into somebody's life and give him or her what the bright Paul Tillich called 'the courage to be.'"[1] Our words have the power to create an environment for our spouses to bravely pursue whatever it is God has called them to be and do. But unfortunately, they also hold the power to hinder and suffocate the courage it takes to do the hard things, the brave things, and the big things. Our words are positive or negative, but rarely are they benign.

This week we will focus on what God's Word teaches us about how He makes us into people of courage and how we can use our words to encourage our spouses to be people of courage.

NOTES

REVIEW

1. Which day of study was the most meaningful to you? Why?

2. What does it mean to be made in the image of God? How could misunderstanding this concept damage a marriage?

Putting 1 First

3. How is a marriage like the relationship between Christ and the church? *1) Never Leaves us Always COMMITTED*

4. Before this study, how would you have defined or described love? How much of your definition was defined by non-biblical influences? Explain.

always loyal

5. Of the characteristics of love listed in 1 Corinthians 13, which one resonates most with you? Which one do you need to work on the most? *Love Is Supportive*

6. Explain why it's so important to embrace the permanence of marriage. *To get away from Easy divace*

7. Why is it so important to understand how much God loves you to be able to truly love your spouse? *Never gives up*

8. Did you do one of the Date Night ideas? If so, share about your experience.

WATCH THE VIDEO

#COMPLEMENTSTUDY

[handwritten top: Catch / Cheered me on]

[handwritten top right: Encourage my spouse / Phil 4:8 / Treasure in your spouse]

DISCUSS

1. What part of the video really got your attention? Why?

2. What does it mean to you to place courage in someone? *[handwritten: Believe in me]*

3. When in your life has someone placed courage in you? *[handwritten: Director]*

4. What hinders you from placing courage in your spouse?

5. Why is it so important that you speak highly of your spouse in private and in public? *[handwritten: wife needs to hear more often]*

6. Why is it so important that spouses encourage one another? *[handwritten: Pray that you mean it]*

7. How are you currently cheering your spouse on to be all God wants him/her to be? *[handwritten: Need to do More]*

8. What's one way right now you can place courage in your spouse?

[handwritten: Count others better than yourselves / Lag down your self for others / Be a servant]

DAY

BECOMING A PERSON OF COURAGE

Father,
Help me to believe I am no longer defined by who I used to be or the sins I still struggle with today. Help me to believe that I am a new creation in Christ Jesus. Tune my heart to the truth and counsel and wisdom of the Holy Spirit dwelling within me. Help me to live out the courage You have poured into me.
Amen

GOD GIVES US A NEW IDENTITY.

At some point in your life, you will ask the questions: *Who am I? What am I here for?* How you answer those questions forms your identity. Your identity reflects who you are and what you value. But as we learned last week, sin shapes what you value and distorts your ability to clearly see who you are. The world is loud. And opinionated. If your true identity reflects who you are—or more aptly whose you are—then you must begin with who God says you are.

When God saves you, not only are you rescued from spending an eternity separated from God, but you become an entirely new creation. God gives His children new identities.

Read 2 Corinthians 5:16-17 in both translations on the next page.

From now on, therefore, we regard no one according to the flesh. Even though we once regarded Christ according to the flesh, we regard him thus no longer. Therefore, if anyone is in Christ, he is a new creation. The old has passed away; behold, the new has come (ESV).	So we have stopped evaluating others from a human point of view. At one time we thought of Christ merely from a human point of view. How differently we know him now! This means that anyone who belongs to Christ has become a new person. The old life is gone; a new life has begun! (NLT)

According to this text, what happens when you belong to
Christ? What happens to your old life?

Using Ephesians 2:1-3 as a guide, write down everything Paul
said you were *before* being saved by the grace of God.
BEFORE CHRIST, I . . .

Scripture says that before you put your faith in Christ, your identity was
as a son or daughter of disobedience or a child of wrath (vv. 2-3). This is
a very real but difficult identifier to believe about yourself.

But because of who God is, that is no longer who you are. In Christ Jesus
you are a new creation—a brand new person! You are no longer identified,
nor should you identify, as the person you used to be. However, Satan still
wants you to believe the lies that you haven't changed, that you can't ever
or won't ever change. He wants you to believe that your sin defines you.

Read 2 Corinthians 5:16-17 again.

How did Paul describe a person who is in Christ? What does it mean to be a new creation? How does being in Christ shape your identity?

Let's take a look at the following verses and write in the adjoining column the defining characteristics of who God says you are. We have done the first one for you.

IN CHRIST, I AM . . .

"For the mountains may depart and the hills be removed, but my steadfast love shall not depart from you, and my covenant of peace shall not be removed," says the LORD, who has compassion on you (Isa. 54:10).	• Loved steadfastly • In a covenant of peace with God • Covered in compassion
But to all who did receive him, who believed in his name, he gave the right to become children of God, who were born, not of blood nor of the will of the flesh nor of the will of man, but of God (John 1:12-13).	
I do not call you servants anymore, because a servant doesn't know what his master is doing. I have called you friends, because I have made known to you everything I have heard from my Father (John 15:15, CSB).	

There is therefore now no condemnation for those who are in
Christ Jesus (Rom. 8:1).

No condemnation

No, in all these things we are
[more than conquerors] through
him who loved us (Rom. 8:37).

Therefore, we are [ambassadors
for Christ,] God making his
appeal through us (2 Cor. 5:20a).

Ambassadors for K

For our sake he made him to be
sin who knew no sin, so that in
him we might become the righteousness of God]2 Cor. 5:21).

For we are his workmanship,
created in Christ Jesus for good
works, which God prepared
beforehand, that we should walk
in them (Eph. 2:10).

*we are
G's workmanship*

(This list is not exhaustive. Many other passages declare who God says you
are. Here are a few more you can check out: John 15:16; Rom. 8:16-17;
1 Cor. 12:27; Eph. 1:7; Phil. 3:20-21; 1 Pet. 2:9-10.)

> Take a moment to let all of these identifiers sink in. You
> are a child of God. You are a friend of God. You are God's
> workmanship. You are redeemed! Justified! You are the
> righteousness of God in Christ Jesus. This is who you are—
> who you truly are in Christ.

CONNECTION POINT

Discuss your answers to these questions together.

Which of these identifiers is most difficult for you to believe? What lies or narratives make it difficult for you to believe this is who you are?

How does having a new identity fuel you with courage to:

- Love and obey God?
- Love your spouse?
- Do the hard thing?

GOD GIVES US HIS HOLY SPIRIT.

A *rauti* was considered a position of dignity and honor among the Tahitian warriors. "The task of the *rauti* is to run alongside men as they charge into battle, and to keep up their courage by reminding them of who they are. The *rauti* sings out the bloodlines and the lineage of each man, reminding the warriors of the glory of their family history. He ensures that they do not forget the heroism of their forefathers."[2]

The first time I read this, I thought—*Man. I wish I had a* rauti *to help me, to encourage me, and to remind me of true things.* And then it hit me—I have something better. All Christians do. We have the Holy Spirit.

Read John 15:26 to learn about our better Helper.

How did Jesus describe the Holy Spirit? How does this title encourage you about the type of counsel and encouragement you are promised to receive from Him?

Who does the Holy Spirit bear witness/testify about? What does this mean?

The Holy Spirit did not come to proclaim Himself or His own agenda, but He came to point people to Jesus—which, if you read on in verse 27, is also our mission. In John 16 Jesus told the disciples it was better for them that He go because if He didn't, the Helper would not come to dwell within them (and us).

Look up the following passages. Write down what you see the Holy Spirit doing in the life of a believer.

John 16:8-13   _Convicts_

Romans 8:26   _Helps in our Weaknesses_

1 Corinthians 2:12-13   _" us understand the Bible_

CONNECTION POINT

Discuss your thoughts on this exercise together.

Share with your spouse about a time when you felt the Holy Spirit guide you into truth, empower you to boldly obey, or convict you of sin. If you cannot think of a recent instance, spend time praying together, asking the Holy Spirit to move you to courageously love and obey Him.

GOD GIVES US HIS WORD.

In salvation, we are made new through Christ Jesus. We are no longer who we once were. But the truth is that while God sees us through the lens of His Son, we often struggle to believe that's who we really are. Most days, we feel stuck, still struggling to untangle ourselves from the habits of sin. The slow work of living out our true identity is called *sanctification.*

God gives us His Word to teach us what His Son is like and how we become like Him. Or, as Howard Hendricks said, "The goal is not to make you a smarter sinner but to make you like the Saviour."[4] We learn how Jesus held fast to truth, how He submitted His life and will to His Father, how He loved and honored people, and how He endured and encouraged His disciples. The Holy Spirit confirms the truth we read in God's Word. When we submit to the Word of God, we experience transformation and change.

In sanctification God sees us for who we are in Christ and slowly and surely conforms us to the image of His Son. He transforms the way we think, believe, and act. We are His workmanship. God begins the work of saving, healing, and transforming us, and God promises to complete it (Phil. 1:6).

Read Isaiah 64:8.

If God is doing the work, what is our responsibility in the process of sanctification?

OBEDience

What do you think it looks like to be clay in the hands of your Father? Be specific.

INTICIPatin g His work on us

As we submit ourselves to God, He sanctifies us by His power, His Spirit, and His Word. He enables and empowers us to love Him and others courageously.

What are some ways you have felt compelled to step into
a radical relationship with God that fear has kept you from doing?

WITNESSING

Spend time asking God to remind you of His presence and power
to fuel you with the courage you need to live and love boldly.

AS YOU GO

Remember this truth: "Therefore, if anyone is in Christ, he is a new
creation. The old has passed away; behold, the new has come" (2 Cor. 5:17).

Fight for this truth: The gospel of Jesus Christ is written on the hearts of
His sons and daughters. The Holy Spirit dwells within us, reminding us that
our identity has been bought and transformed by the blood of Jesus Christ.

He is our better Helper. The Holy Spirit comforts us and strengthens us.
He whispers truth, convicts us with truth, and provides wisdom to live out
that truth. He is our constant Source of courage.

Pray this truth: *God, thank You for Your Word. Thank You for*
teaching me . . . *what to do, to lean on you, to*
step out believing you will come
thru

Help me to trust and obey You with . . .

Amen

DAY

ENCOURAGED
TO GIVE
COURAGE

Father,
Help me to live out my God-given identity
as a new creation, full of courage, full
of power, and full of love to love those
around me. Help me place courage in
others through my prayers for them and
my words to them.
Amen

Some of the ways God places courage in us is through the encouragement, counsel, and wisdom of fellow believers. If you recall, before Paul was the apostle of great faith who wrote two-thirds of the New Testament, he was a murderer with a particular vendetta against Christians. But God stopped him in his tracks and changed his life forever (Acts 9:1-9). God used a fellow believer named Ananias to help Paul.

Read Acts 9:10-19.

Can you imagine the fear Ananias must have felt? God called him to put himself within arms reach of a man who had the authority of the chief priests to kill him.

What did God say to Ananias that gave him the courage to obey (v. 15)?

To *encourage* means to inspire with courage, to embolden, and to spur on.[5]

God uses our brothers and sisters in Christ to encourage us. Look at the legacy of placing courage that started generations before us:

- God placed courage in Ananias to minister to a murderer.

- Ananias placed courage in Paul.

- Paul spent the rest of his life placing courage in the churches by building them up through prayers and words.

PRAYER THAT BUILDS UP

Our lives should be marked by wisdom, knowledge, truth, discernment, and love. But we also need courage to live out said wisdom, knowledge, truth, discernment, and love. Christians are to have an undivided and loyal heart toward King Jesus. However, we would be ignorant to believe our loyalty will go unchallenged. Everything—including our own desires, culture, and Satan—is vying to own and control the attention and affections of our hearts. It requires courage to follow the way of Jesus.

I can think of no better illustration showing the need for Christian courage than what took place in the garden of Gethsemane. Jesus knew this day was coming—the day He would surrender His spirit and body to secure the hope of salvation for the world. But Jesus wasn't leaping up onto the cross with His superhero cape on. He was lying facedown in the garden, sweating anxious drops of blood, begging His Father to provide a different way. John Onwuchekwa wrote, "Jesus stared death square in the eyes, knowing his fate was inescapable. How did he face it? On his knees in prayer."[6]

> What is something you currently need courage for? To face a day of difficult parenting? To love your spouse in a difficult season? To share the gospel with a neighbor? Write it below.

You can do what God has called you to do, what is difficult, and what is scary because Christ strengthens you. He is our courage.

Take a moment to write a prayer, asking God to give you faith to believe the power of Christ in you to face whatever comes your way today.

Paul implored us to imitate him as he imitated Christ (1 Cor. 11:1). One way Paul imitated Jesus was by praying for those he cared for to have faith that would not fail (Luke 22:31-32). If you want to know how Paul felt about the people of God, look no further than his prayers. Paul prayed for God to pour courage into his partners in the faith. We want to imitate Paul in his passion to pray for courage in the people he cared about.

Read the following passages and then write a prayer for you to share with your spouse. Be specific as you seek the Lord on his/her behalf.

PRAYER FOR KNOWLEDGE OF GOD

Read Ephesians 1:16-19.

How did Paul describe the Spirit?

What did Paul pray they would know? Why is it important your spouse knows these things?

Rewrite Ephesians 1:16-19 as a personal prayer for your spouse.

PRAYER FOR STRENGTH AND POWER

Read Ephesians 3:14-21.

What did Paul pray they would be strengthened with? How? Where? Why?

What did Paul pray they would be able to comprehend? Why does your spouse need to comprehend this?

Rewrite Ephesians 3:14-21 as a personal prayer for your spouse.

PRAYER FOR LOVE TO ABOUND

Read Philippians 1:9-11.

What did Paul want their love to grow in?

Why is it important for your spouse's love to grow in this way?

Rewrite Philippians 1:9-11 as a personal prayer for your spouse.

PRAYER TO BEAR FRUIT

Read Colossians 1:9-14.

Why did Paul pray they would "walk in a manner worthy of the Lord" (v. 10)? What does that mean?

What does it mean to bear "fruit in every good work" (v. 10)?

In what ways do you want to see your spouse bear fruit?

Relatives coming to KT

Rewrite Colossians 1:9-14 as a prayer for your spouse.

Prayer is powerful. More than anything we can say to one another, the words we pray to God are the words that matter most. God doesn't respond to our prayers because of our words but because of His character—His mercy, grace, love, and faithfulness. Praying for your spouse is a priority. It shows you are for him/her.

WORDS THAT BUILD UP

If we are praying for our spouses, is it right for us to affirm them and cheer them on verbally? I mean, if we affirm them, aren't we merely encouraging them to be puffed up in pride?

In Matthew 25:21,23 the master told the workers who made good use of their talents, "Well done, good and faithful servant."

Isn't this what we all want to hear at the end of our lives—"Well done, good and faithful servant"? We inherently desire approval and praise. The problem is not in the desire to be encouraged and cheered on. The problem is when we seek the approval of people over God.

Read what Sam Crabtree wrote in **Practicing Affirmation** *on the following page.*

*Affirming Christlike transformation makes
a distinction between praising a doer of good and
praising a do-gooder. One commends the pursuit
of that which is truly excellent; the other flatters
the performer who longs to outdo others, seeking
attention and man's applause. . . . To affirm
Christlikeness in transformed believers is to affirm
what Christ purchased with his own blood. He
did not spill his blood for the church because she
was worth it; his blood, spilled for her, establishes
her worth.*[7]

Just as God speaks words to us that build up, inspire, refresh, and restore, we are to speak words to our spouses that do the same for them.

Read Proverbs 18:21 and Ephesians 4:29.

Consider what type of words you are speaking over your spouse. Are your words imitating God's? Are they speaking life or death? Are they building up or tearing down? Explain.

In Philemon 1:4-7 Paul praised Philemon because of the way he refreshed the hearts of the saints. To be *refreshed* means to have "restor[ed] strength."[8] It's a glass of cold water on a hot day.

Consider how you speak to your spouse. Are your words refreshing to your spouse's soul? As the Lord brings to mind words you've spoken that were not refreshing, repent of them to the Lord, then confess to your spouse and seek forgiveness.

Paul prayed for the church, but he also affirmed the people when he saw them doing something really great.

Read the following passages to see how Paul placed courage in the church.

Philippians 2:12—What did Paul see them doing well?

Philippians 4:10-14,18—Why was Paul thankful for the church of Philippi?

1 Thessalonians 5:11—What were the Thessalonicans already doing that Paul encouraged them to continue doing?

Dr. Ian Hamilton wrote, "Encouragers have Christ-like sight and a Christ-like heart. They are not blind to the sins and weaknesses in fellow Christians, but they recognize that 'love builds up.' . . . Encouragers are often our great High Priest's means of ministering his divine sympathy to our bruised and lacerated souls."[9]

CONNECTION POINT

Discuss your answers to these questions together.

We have numerous reasons and ways to encourage those we love. Yet many spouses feel a deficit in affirmation. Sadly, numerous affairs begin because a husband or wife receives more encouragement and affirmation from someone other than his/her spouse. Spend some time processing this with your spouse. Below and on the next page are some questions to consider in your conversation:

On a scale of 1 to 10, with 1 being "Starving for Encouragement," and 10 being "Totally Affirmed," how affirmed or encouraged do you feel from me?

CONNECTION POINT

Discuss your answers to these questions together.

What are some things that cause you to not share words of encouragement with me?

Are there people, other than me, who make you feel more encouraged and affirmed? In what way?

Spend some time praying together and asking God to help your marriage be the relationship where you get and give the most affirmation and encouragement.

AS YOU GO

Remember this truth: "Therefore encourage one another and build one another up, just as you are doing" (1 Thess. 5:11).

Fight for this truth: Your words matter. Your words have the power to build up and encourage your spouse to follow Christ, to do the hard thing, and to know how deeply loved he/she is.

Pray this truth: *God, thank You for Your Word. Thank You for teaching me . . .*

Help me to trust and obey You with . . .

Amen

3

CREATING A
COURAGE-RICH
RELATIONSHIP

Father,
I want my marriage to be a place where
my spouse and I can flourish. Help me to
foster an environment where my spouse
can grow to know You more, feel more
loved by You and me, and be filled with
the courage to fully live out Your calling on
his/her life.
Amen

Today, we are going to work through Hebrews 10:24-25, learning what it means to consider our spouses and how to stir up courage within them.

> *And let us consider how to stir up one another to love and good works, not neglecting to meet together, as is the habit of some, but encouraging one another, and all the more as you see the Day drawing near.*
> **HEBREWS 10:24-25**

CONSIDER.

The writer of Hebrews said we should consider how to stir up one another to love and good works. To *consider* means "to think about carefully."[10]

To be able to stir up your spouse, friend, or neighbor, you have to know him/her. Here are a few tips on how to do that:

ASK QUESTIONS.

Be the most curious person about your spouse that has ever existed. Sincerely desire to know what your spouse thinks about everything, what makes him/her tick and why, what winds him/her up and why, what he/she dreams about, what creates a knot in his/her throat, and on and on.

LISTEN.

Hearing is different from listening. Listening is taking in the words someone is saying and reaching to understand the meaning of those words. Listening takes undivided attention. Put your phone down. Repeat your understanding back to him/her. And if you have mistaken his/her meaning, ask more questions to grow in understanding.

TRULY SEE YOUR SPOUSE.

One of the most powerful verses in Scripture is Matthew 9:35-36:

> *And Jesus went throughout all the cities and villages, teaching in their synagogues and proclaiming the gospel of the kingdom and healing every disease and every affliction. When he saw the crowds, he had compassion for them, because they were harassed and helpless, like sheep without a shepherd.*

Jesus saw the crowds. He didn't just glance their way; He really saw them. He saw their hurts, their needs, their brokenness, and He had compassion for them. We all want to be seen by our spouses. No one wants to feel invisible in his/her marriage. Seeing someone takes intentionality.

Do you see your spouse? What do you see in him/her? What are some ways you can move toward him/her in compassion and care? What are some ways you can place courage in him/her?

Spend a few moments asking God to help you really see your spouse. Write down what God shows you about him/her. Ask God to show you how to mobilize what you see into compassionate action.

STIR UP.

Your words have the power to stir up (provoke feelings or actions in) your spouse. They will either create a negative or a positive environment. Negative words, or even withholding positive words, have the power to provoke insecurity, fear, anxiety, distrust, and loneliness in your spouse. Likewise, encouraging words to your spouse have the power to provoke confidence in who he/she is in Christ, to inspire him/her, and to affirm that he/she can do what God has called him/her to do. Your words—or lack of words—matter in your marriage.

Look up the following verses about the power of what we say. Write them out in your own words, then consider what these words might stir up in your spouse.

	Write out the verse in your own words.	What might these words stir up in your spouse?
Proverbs 12:18		
Proverbs 15:4		
Proverbs 16:24		
Proverbs 25:11		

CONNECTION POINT

Discuss your answers to these questions together.

Think about the conversations you've had with your spouse over the last few days: Have the words spoken between the two of you fostered a courage-rich environment? Explain.

....

....

....

TO LOVE AND GOOD WORKS . . .

Our words should be intended to stir up love and good works. For our marriages to be rich in courage, we have to be intentional to speak words that remind our spouses of both God's love and our love for them. Our words should remind our spouses that God has a plan for their lives (Ps. 139:1-16; Jer. 29:11; Eph. 2:19), and we are here to help them accomplish all that God has called them to do.

EXERCISE: SEVEN DAYS OF WORDS

Hebrews 3:13 says that, as Christians, we are called to exhort one another every day. This activity will give you that opportunity since you will write words of encouragement to your spouse for seven days in a row. Maybe you've done a similar activity before, like tucking a stack of handwritten notes into your spouse's luggage before going on a trip—one for each day he/she is away.

We have provided seven Scriptures and a theme, one for each day of the week. Read the passage and ponder the truth that's there as it relates to your spouse. What ways have you seen your spouse display this attribute or truth? How have you seen your spouse fight sin, cling to truth, and show grace? What is something God is showing you to gracefully caution your spouse about? Use the space provided under each reference for a rough draft. Then, use actual cards to write your spouse a note of encouragement. Give your spouse one note per day for seven days.

1. WORDS OF LOVE AND MERCY
Ephesians 2:4-5

2. WORDS OF EXHORTATION AND STRENGTH
Isaiah 50:4

3. WORDS OF TRUTH AND GRACE
Ephesians 4:29

4. WORDS OF CHEER AND ENCOURAGEMENT
Philippians 4:8

5. WORDS OF CORRECTION AND CAUTION
Colossians 3:16

6. WORDS OF LONGING AND DESIRE
Song of Solomon 1:16a

7. WORDS OF HOPE AND EXPECTATION
Jeremiah 29:11

Was it difficult to write these seven notes? If so, why?

Name some things you can do this week to encourage a courage-rich relationship with your spouse.

 ## *AS YOU GO*

Remember this truth: "And let us consider how to stir up one another to love and good works, not neglecting to meet together, as is the habit of some, but encouraging one another, and all the more as you see the Day drawing near" (Heb. 10:24-25).

Fight for this truth: Your words have the power to provoke your spouse to love and good works. Use your words to echo God's heart for your spouse.

Pray for this truth: *God, thank You for Your Word. Thank You for teaching me . . .*

Help me to trust and obey You with . . .

Amen

DAY

4

TALK
IT OUT

We encourage you to take a few minutes on this day to sit with your spouse and process what you studied this week. Use some or all of the following questions to guide your discussion:

1. Which day of study was your favorite and why?

2. What was the most difficult portion of the study for you and why?

3. How is our marriage healthier if we both understand who we are in Christ?

4. How do you see me growing in my spiritual life? What can I do to encourage you in your walk with Christ?

5. How can I best pray for you right now?

6. How can we better use our words to build each other up?

7. What can I do to be a better listener?

8. Would you say we have a courage-rich relationship? Why or why not? What can we do to champion that kind of environment?

9. Which of the "As You Go" statements really captured your heart? Why?

Finish this day by praying together. Take time to list some specific requests you can pray for over each other. Then, spend some time praying about other areas of your marriage God has revealed to you that need attention or refining.

It's so important that you and your spouse spend quality time together on a consistent basis. You'll need to be purposeful and intentional to make this happen. We want to help. Each week we'll provide one or two simple date night ideas. Of course, "date night" could be a "date morning" or "date afternoon." Whatever best fits your schedule. And if you're wondering what to talk about, feel free to use the designated connection points found throughout this week's study or the discussion questions found on Day 4.

DATE IDEAS FOR THIS WEEK

1. Since we've talked a lot about words this week, head to your local library as a part of this date. Each of you take a few minutes to search the library to find five book titles that describe how you feel about your spouse. They can be serious or lighthearted, just not derogatory. Find a table together and share each book title and why you chose it.

2. Sticking with the words theme, go to a store that carries greeting cards. Each of you choose two cards—one serious and one humorous—that you might buy your spouse to express your feelings toward him/her. Once you both have selected the cards, reveal to your spouse what you selected and why. Then, put the cards back in their places and go grab a coffee or some ice cream together.

FOLLOW
AND LEAD

#COMPLEMENTSTUDY

Mutual submission is one of the defining marks of a Christ-follower. Submission is the absolute surrender of our lives, preferences, wills, and desires. True submission has to be given—it can never be taken. And, interestingly enough, the result of true submission is freedom.

Richard J. Foster said the corresponding freedom to the discipline of mutual submission "is the ability to lay down the terrible burden of always needing to get our own way. . . . In submission we are at last free to value other people."[1]

> *TRUE SUBMISSION HAS TO BE GIVEN— IT CAN NEVER BE TAKEN.*

This idea of mutual submission is why God's vision of marriage was so stunning to the first church. Marriage in the first century was transactional, simply a pre-planned arrangement. It was often void of love, sacrifice, and affection. God's view of marriage would have been incredibly countercultural.

Although God intends for submission to be beautifully framed in the context of marriage, we know that marriages, more than any other relationships, suffer the most damage from a misunderstood and abusive concept of submission. But Scripture shows that mutual submission produces freedom and value for God's image bearers. That's why we are talking about this today. We pray in hope that this concept is reclaimed so relationships, marriages, and the church body can experience a revival of love, value, and freedom as we collectively surrender in mutual submission to each other under the lordship and leadership of Jesus Christ.

One of the most beautifully confounding things about Jesus is that although He is God and King, He spent His time on earth shedding His equality with God and taking up a life of service and submission. In the Gospel of John alone, Jesus acted under the will of His Father forty-seven times.[2] "I can do nothing on my own," Jesus stated. "As I hear, I judge, and my judgment is just, because I seek not my own will but the will of him who sent me" (John 5:30).

Jesus willfully submitted to His Father, to the Holy Scriptures, and to earthly authorities. Though He was God, He didn't live His life as you might think a God-King would. His life was marked by servanthood and sacrifice. He shared with the marginalized and oppressed and lifted the value and status of women. Jesus was radically counter-cultural.

And it is Jesus whom we are called to imitate as we walk in love and "submit to one another . . ." (Eph. 5:21a, NLT). Our marriages should be marked by radically counter-cultural servanthood and sacrifice. This week we are going to look at what it means to submit to one another out of reverence to Christ.

NOTES

REVIEW

1. Which day of study was the most meaningful to you? Why?

2. Who is someone that has really encouraged you?

3. How do you respond to the definition of encouragement as "placing courage in someone"? Does that make sense to you? Explain.

4. Which of the passages about who you are in Christ on pages 54–55 really resonated with you? Why?

5. Why is understanding who you are in Christ essential in having a godly, flourishing marriage?

6. Do you and your spouse pray for each other? Do you pray with each other? Why are both needed?

7. Why are encouraging words so important in your marriage? Would you say you're a good encourager? Why or why not?

8. What are you currently doing to foster a courage-rich environment in your marriage?

9. Did you do one of the Date Night ideas? If so, share about your experience.

WATCH THE VIDEO

DISCUSS

1. What part of the video really got your attention? Why?

2. Are you comfortable talking about leading and following in a marriage? Why or why not? Why is this discussion so countercultural?

3. Why do you think the word *submission* gets such a bad rap? Have you ever viewed the word negatively? Explain.

4. Why are the best leaders those who choose to walk side-by-side with you? Why is this concept so important in the marriage relationship?

5. Can a husband and wife both take part in leading the family? What does that look like? How has that happened in your marriage?

6. Why is understanding the concept of leading and following so important to your marriage?

7. Would you say that Jesus is the ultimate Leader of your home? Why or why not? What needs to change for that to be the case?

DAY

IMITATING CHRIST IN THE WAY OF LOVE

Father,
Help me today as I study Your Word. May Your truth be the light that guides me through the complexities, nuances, and cultural ideas that attempt to choke out understanding. Help me believe that surrendering to Your idea of submission will only bring about more joy in my life. Amen

Today, we take a close look at the principles of marriage contained in Ephesians 5. Paul's description of marriage in this passage has been misunderstood and misapplied, leaving a mess of confused and hurting men and women in its wake. As Dr. Russell Moore explained, "Part of this is because we tend to define what the Bible calls submission and headship in terms of power rather than in terms of the cross."[3]

Read Ephesians 5:21-33.

Consider how you currently view this passage. Do you tend to define the marital roles of husband and wife in terms of power? Explain.

How might seeing our roles in terms of power wrongly affect the way we treat one another in our marriages?

Read Galatians 3:23-29.

The cross of Jesus Christ is the great equalizer. "There is neither Jew nor Greek, slave nor free, male nor female—for [we] are all one in Christ Jesus" (v. 28, BSB).

> How do you see the cross making the dignity and value of all people equal?

MUTUAL SUBMISSION

Read Ephesians 5:1-2. Two commands are in this verse.

1. Be _____ of God.

2. Walk in _____.

To "walk in love" was Paul's broad response to a myriad of specific questions—*How should I treat my neighbor? Walk in love as Christ loved us. How should I treat my wife? Walk in love as Christ loved us. What should I say to defend myself? Walk in love as Christ loved us.* The command is broad, but the principle is specific and narrow—walk in love as Christ loved us.

Jesus loved the world by sacrificing His life in obedience to the Father.

All of our love for people, especially our spouses, should flow from this same principle. Walking in love might look like sacrifice, or it might look like honoring someone over yourself or laying down your preferences. It might look like leading, or it might look like following. And, according to Ephesians 5:21, walking in love looks like submission.

SUBMIT *(HYPOTASSŌ):* TO SUBORDINATE; TO SUBMIT TO ONE'S CONTROL; TO YIELD TO ONE'S ADMONITION OR ADVICE

"This word was a Greek military term meaning 'to arrange [troop divisions] in a military fashion under the command of a leader.' In non-military use, it was 'a voluntary attitude of giving in, cooperating, assuming responsibility, and carrying a burden.'"[4]

> What does it mean to submit to one another out of reverence for (in the fear of) Christ?

The willingness and ability for us to submit to one another is empowered by the Holy Spirit's presence in our lives (v. 18) and motivated by our recognition that Christ is Lord. Reading on in Ephesians 6, this applies to other relationships besides the marital one. And in all of those relationships, we need to keep in mind that submission is not speaking to the order of authority but the operation of it—how submission is given and received. It's not about throwing your weight around but living with a servant heart.[5]

Specifically, for our purposes in this study, let's narrow this submission conversation to marriage.

> What does it look like for a husband and wife to submit to one another?

> How is choosing to submit in marriage a manifestation of love?

CONNECTION POINT

Discuss your answers to these questions together.

What is your most obvious barrier to considering your spouse more significant than yourself? What hinders you from taking the steps to repent and begin tearing down this barrier?

....

....

....

Read Matthew 11:28-29 and Mark 8:34-36.

What did Jesus ask us to take up in each of these passages?

Both of these items seem heavy and burdensome, but they actually lead to freedom and rest. How so?

In the Mark 8 passage, denying yourself and laying down your life means you are free to pick up the cross of Jesus Christ and follow Him into eternal life. Jesus said for us to gain, we have to lose.

In Matthew 11:29 Jesus says, "Take my yoke upon you." A yoke is a heavy piece of wood that binds an older, stronger ox with a younger, smaller ox. The bigger ox carries all the weight of the yoke, thereby freeing the smaller ox to learn the art of farming without any burden.[6]

Jesus' commands feel counter-intuitive, but they are true.

How does taking up Jesus' cross and taking on Jesus' yoke free you to value your spouse more significantly than yourself?

The world says we will experience more love, power, freedom, and significance when others are submissive to us. But God says we will experience more love, power, freedom, and significance when we submit ourselves to one another.

Remembering that your actions reveal your heart, which of these two messages do your actions show you believe?

If the previous question brings conviction about how you have wrongly treated others, especially your spouse, spend a few moments in prayer and repentance. Then, ask the Holy Spirit to continually remind you that mutual submission is the way of love.

HEADSHIP AND SUBMISSION

The biblical concepts of headship and submission in marriage are incredibly controversial. What does it mean that a husband is called to headship and a wife is called to submission to her husband? Dr. Moore brought clarity to the topic:

> The message that we, as redeemed sinners, will reign with Christ is all about what it means to have been conformed to him through the sanctifying of our minds, our souls, our affections, our wills. The reign of believers with Christ is not akin to that of a city council meeting, with debates and filibusters and compromises. The Head is seamless from the body. We share the mind of Christ (1 Cor. 2:16). His purposes are now our purposes; his priorities are now our priorities. This differs, of course, from the sort of unity we see in a marriage, because Jesus is the sinless Lord, and none of us are. We do not have dominion over one another, even when we are responsible to lead. The point though is that this sort of joint-reign is possible because of organic unity. Hierarchy and mutuality are not opposed to one another. Submission, then, in Ephesians 5 and elsewhere is not presented in terms of unblinking obedience but in terms of seeking to respect and to cultivate the spiritual accountability of one's husband. The controversial part of this passage to those who first heard it would not be submission and headship but rather how the gospel radically redefined those terms and limited them.[7]

WHAT SUBMISSION AND HEADSHIP ARE NOT

A WIFE'S SUBMISSION **IS NOT**	A HUSBAND'S HEADSHIP **IS NOT**
submitting to all men;	dominion or power over his wife;
unwavering obedience to her husband;	disengagement or passivity in responsibility;
docility or servitude.	making decisions in isolation.

WHAT SUBMISSION AND HEADSHIP ARE

A WIFE'S SUBMISSION **IS**	A HUSBAND'S HEADSHIP **IS**
sacrifice and service in the imitation of Christ;	sacrifice and service in the imitation of Christ;
a voluntary attitude of recognition toward her husband's godly leadership;	putting his wife's needs above his own;
respecting God's call to give spiritual accountability to her own husband.	accountability for the spiritual direction of his family.

The late Vickie Kraft explained mutual submission like this:

> *Biblical marriage requires mutual submission. Yes,*
> *the wife yields her rights and submits to her husband's*
> *leadership. But the husband is to yield his rights to*
> *independence, to controlling all the money, and to*
> *making all the decisions. He is to recognize that he is*
> *married to a woman who is one flesh with him.*
>
> *For some men, this is a difficult assignment and a big*
> *issue. It is very hard for a man to sacrificially give up*
> *his own rights for the sake of his wife. And yet God*
> *requires an unselfish love that seeks the woman's*
> *highest good, with no hint of her husband lording*
> *it over her. This view of marriage is distinctively*
> *Christian, an expression of God's love acted out*
> *through the control of the Spirit.*
>
> *As a matter of fact, Christian marriages were*
> *astonishing to the Roman world. In a society where*
> *women had no rights, here was wifely submission*
> *balanced by loving sacrificial headship. Marriage*
> *was placed on a very firm basis of mutuality,*
> *with both partners having equal rights. Such an*
> *arrangement was revolutionary in that day.*[8]

Mutual submission produces freedom in marriage. When the husband and wife are each trying to outdo one another with honor and do everything they can to encourage and develop the strengths and gifts of their spouses, a marriage can't help but thrive.

What are some ways you have misunderstood your role as husband or wife?

Imagine a couple walking in an ideal relationship of mutual submission. Describe what that might look like.

Spend some time processing the concept of submission and headship with your spouse. What ways do you want to see your marriage grow in love and mutual submission?

 *AS YOU GO*

Remember this truth: "Do nothing from selfish ambition or conceit, but in humility count others more significant than yourselves" (Phil. 2:3).

Fight for this truth: A marriage built on mutual submission will reflect the glory, love, and sacrifice of the cross of Jesus Christ.

Pray this truth: *God, thank You for Your Word. Thank You for teaching me . . .*

Help me to trust and obey You with . . .

Amen

FOLLOWING LIKE A LEADER

Jesus,

You are my Leader. You lead me in the way of love and compassionate care for all people. Teach me to be a servant-leader, an honor-giver, and a joyful-obeyer. Help me to follow You in the way of love. Take away my selfish desires that conflict with the holy desire to lay my life down for others the way You laid Your life down for me. Amen

WHEN IT COMES TO THE WORD *SUBMISSION*, HERE'S WHAT WE KNOW:

. . . people have experienced a lot of pain because of this word;

. . . the church has not always done a great job of teaching or exemplifying the biblical meaning of the word;

. . . men and women alike have wrongly handled this word;

. . . pastors and teachers and other leaders have misused and abused this word;

. . . there is a cultural and political firestorm around this very word.

We are aware. Yet we are talking about it anyway. Why?

We believe living in the biblical meaning of submission results in a beautiful, powerful experience.

We believe that God can heal what was wounded or broken through a misunderstanding or abuse of this word.

Jesus is our example of a person who submitted His whole person—soul and body—to the wisdom and way of His Father. This is the calling of a disciple of Christ.

And we believe that marriages, other relationships, and the church body could experience a revival of love if we collectively surrendered to God's desire for each of us to submit to the lordship and leadership of Jesus Christ.

RULING OVER OUR DESIRES

One of the greatest relational consequences for Adam and Eve's sin was the distortion of desire. God filled His first creations with good desire—a passionate longing to experience pleasure, joy, and rest—with God the Father, God the Son, and God the Spirit. He invited humanity to experience pure and harmonious relational bliss with each other and with the Godhead. But sin damaged and distorted the desires of our souls. Because of sin, the cycle of man and woman outdoing one another with love and honor looks more like the kid's hand-stacking game—each of us trying to get our hand on top of the others.

Let's first look at the consequences sin has on our desires. Then, we'll spend the rest of our time seeing how we can rule over our wrong desires.

Read Genesis 3:16 and Genesis 4:7.

> *To the woman he said,*
> *"I will surely multiply your pain in childbearing;*
> *in pain you shall bring forth children.*
> *Your desire shall be contrary to your husband,*
> *but he shall rule over you."*
> **GENESIS 3:16**

> *. . . sin is crouching at the door. Its desire is for you, but*
> *you must rule over it.*
> **GENESIS 4:7b, CSB**

This specific Hebrew word for *desire* is used only three times in Scripture. It means "stretching out after; a longing."[9]

> Who does the desire belong to in Genesis 3:16? What is the
> object of her desire?

The meaning of the last statement in verse 16 provokes much debate. But one thing seems certain: Eve's desire will lead to conflict and struggle in the marriage relationship.

> Who/what does the desire belong to in Genesis 4:7? What is
> the object of its desire?

> What did God say we should do to the sin that is crouching at our door?

Desire is a powerful thing. James 1:15 says,

> *Then desire when it has conceived gives birth to sin,*
> *and sin when it is fully grown brings forth death.*

We naturally obey our desires—we're hungry, so we eat; we're tired, so we sleep. But when our desires begin to rule us, and we stretch out after something that is contrary to God's Word, He tells us we are to rule over our desires.

Paul wrote,

> *Don't be a slave of your desires or live like people who*
> *don't know God.*
>
> **1 THESSALONIANS 4:5, CEV**

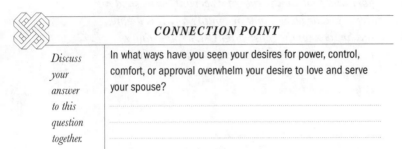

CONNECTION POINT

Discuss	In what ways have you seen your desires for power, control,
your	comfort, or approval overwhelm your desire to love and serve
answer	your spouse?
to this	
question	
together.	

How can you put to death the desires of your flesh so that you can mutually submit to your spouse in sacrificial love?

Because of Jesus, we are no longer slaves to our desires. And because of Jesus, we are free to live out God's original intention for harmonious and honorable relationships. Within the context of marriage, this means we can choose to rule over our desires so we might experience a more freeing, flourishing, and unified relationship.

Restoring a right relationship within our marriages means we must learn to rule over our desires that challenge the call to submit our whole personhood to Jesus and to show our reverence to Jesus by submitting to one another. Doing so will reflect our obedience to the Great Commandment—loving God more than anything and, secondly, loving our neighbor to the same degree we love ourselves (Matt. 22:36-40).

THE DANCE

In their book, *The Meaning of Marriage*, Dr. Timothy and Kathy Keller describe the beautiful relationship between the Father and the Son in the Godhead.

> *Jesus was equal with God, he emptied himself of his*
> *glory and took on the role of a servant. Jesus shed his*
> *divine privileges without becoming any less divine,*
> *and he took on the most submissive role—that of*
> *a servant who dies in his master's service. . . . Jesus's*
> *willing acceptance of this role was wholly voluntary,*
> *a gift to his Father.*

To this, Kathy asked herself the question:

> *If it was not an assault on the dignity and divinity*
> *(but rather led to the greater glory) of the Second*
> *Person of the Godhead to submit himself, and assume*
> *the role of a servant, then how could it possibly injure*
> *me to be asked to play out the "Jesus role" in my*
> *marriage?*[10]

Husband, in your own words, what does it mean to fulfill the "Jesus role" in your marriage?

How are you currently fulfilling this role?

What ways have you struggled to serve your family in this way?

Wife, in your own words, what does it mean to fulfill the "Jesus role" in your marriage?

How are you currently fulfilling this role?

What ways have you struggled to serve your family in this way?

One might ask—why did God give man the role of leader and woman the role of helper? The most honest answer we can give is . . . we don't know. We understand the importance of a leader role and a helper role and agree that men and women are equal in dignity, worth, and value. We also recognize that God necessitated both men and women working together to fully represent His love to the world. Consider the Kellers' thoughts on this question:

> . . . rigid cultural gender roles have no Biblical warrant. Christians cannot make a scriptural case for masculine and feminine stereotypes. Though social scientists have made good cases about abiding gender differences with regard to the expression of emotion, . . . different individual personalities and different cultures will express those distinctions in somewhat different ways. . . . We must find ways to honor and express our gender roles, but the Bible allows for freedom in the particulars, while still upholding the obligatory nature of the principle.[11]

Scripture is not vague or silent on things that we need to know details about. However, when it is quiet on an issue, it is best to operate in wisdom and discernment. We often consider leadership in terms of a hierarchy. But for us to navigate the complexities of God's design for leadership in a marriage, we have to understand where we are going. Think back to our first week of study. The purpose of marriage is to show the world God's unbreakable love for humanity. The aim of the leader is to lead the marriage to accomplish this purpose.

How do you decide who leads in what situations? How do you maximize the gifts, skills, and wisdom of both spouses in a marriage? Husbands and wives are both called to lead in different ways and in different times in marriage. Decision-making can be a beautiful way to see how God has brought two people with different gifts, abilities, and personalities together in one flesh for the common good.

Here are a few questions we've found helpful as we navigate making decisions in our home:

Who has the most knowledge or insight about this specific situation?

Whose giftings apply most directly to the decision?

Whose personality is most suited for leadership in this decision?

Consider the biggest decisions you and your spouse have worked through or are currently facing. How can questions like this be helpful?

AS YOU GO

Remember this truth: "Don't be a slave of your desires or live like people who don't know God" (1 Thess. 4:5, CEV).

Fight for this truth: Jesus is the ultimate leader who is worthy of following, submitting to, and loving with my whole heart.

Pray for this truth: *God, thank You for Your Word. Thank You for teaching me . . .*

Help me to trust and obey You with . . .

Amen

DAY

GIVING TRUST

"Heavenly Father,
let the morning, but *also* the noon and
night bring us word of your unfailing love;
for your love is better than life, your
faithfulness the heartbeat of our hope,
and your word the foundation of all trust.
We come—we run to you this day seeking
help. We lift our hands to you in adoring
love and earnest anticipation. Show us
the way forward."[12]
Amen

In our marriages, we're going to fail one another daily.
It's not because we don't try to love one another well or
surrender ourselves to mutual submission. It's not that we
don't want to see our spouses thrive and flourish. But try and
try as we might, some days we just get it wrong. We won't
lead well. We won't do a good job of supporting one another.
We'll fail at mutually submitting. We won't love one another
well. We won't even be nice to one another. It's in these
moments our trust in one another begins to fracture.

If we let those fractures go untended, they will eventually
morph into full-blown breaks. Trusting our spouses can feel
impossible at times. But how do we give trust to our spouses
when they have broken our trust?

NEW MORNING MERCIES

We must not fail to see, really see, the meaning of the
morning. God breaks the darkness with the miracle of
morning to remind us that darkness is bound by His
sovereignty. The night comes with persistence, but the day

breaks through with an unchanging, promising, and powerful reliability. God demonstrates His inexhaustible and indomitable love for you through every rising sun.

Read the following passages:

- Psalm 30:4-5

- Psalm 90:14

- Psalm 143:8

- Lamentations 3:22-24

What are the commonalities in all of these passages?

Eugene Peterson said this about the morning light:

> *The creative action of God is light, which encloses and limits a temporary darkness. . . . The shadows are there—night descends upon life—and there is that which seems to defy God, to disturb his order and his purpose: sickness, death, trouble, and sorrow. But it does not have the last word: "And there was morning, one day."[13]*

The prophet Jeremiah praised the Lord for His steadfast love and mercy (Lam. 3:23-24). Just as the sun will not fail to rise in the morning, God's mercies will not fail us.

How might considering the new mercies you receive every morning compel you to give new mercies to your spouse?

According to Psalm 30:5, how long does God's anger last? What did the psalmist say lasts forever?

God's anger is completely pure and righteous. Yet even God's anger only lasts but a moment.

What does this comparison between God's anger and God's favor compel you to do with your anger—whether you feel it's justified or not? Why?

Don't let darkness, anger, hurt, and brokenness have the last word in your marriage. Spend some time processing how to let the morning light breathe new mercies, forgiveness, and love into areas of broken trust.

Just as Jesus foretold, Peter denied his Friend and King three times before Jesus died. Peter was crushed under the guilt and shame of betraying Jesus during His time of need. But that's not the end of the story. The third time Jesus revealed Himself to the disciples after His resurrection, Peter experienced new mercies.

Read the account of Jesus and Peter reconciling their relationship in John 21:1-19.

Who was pursuing reconciliation for who in this story?

Peter promised to never deny Jesus, but he broke trust with Him when he failed to keep this promise.

Do you resonate with this type of heartbreaking failure? In what way?

We have all been the one to break trust and fail someone we love.

How does Jesus' mercy and grace toward Peter remind you of His mercy and grace toward you?

Read verses 15-19 again.

Peter denied Jesus three times. Then Jesus restored Peter three times.

Read the following commentary from the **ESV Gospel Transformation Study Bible** *on the power of this moment:*

> *Gospel surgery is free, but not always easy. Grace produces redemptive pain, not punitive pain. But pain is still painful. Indeed, the gospel brings an end to all deadening worldly grief. But the gospel is the beginning of enlivening godly grief (2 Cor. 7:10-11). The law condemns, the gospel convicts; the law creates self-centered tears, the gospel creates God-centered tears.*
>
> *"Do you love me more than these?" It would have been easier on Peter had Jesus asked him, "Do you promise not to fail me again?" But Jesus knew better than to ask that question, because, of course, Peter would fail again (e.g., Gal. 2:11-21). Jesus is more jealous for our love than zealous for our works. If he has our hearts, he'll have everything else.[14]*

Discuss your answers to these questions together.

Consider a situation that created broken trust between you and your spouse. What would it look like to apply gospel grace and new morning mercies to this situation?

When your spouse has broken your trust, do you offer restorative trust or demand him/her to feel punitive pain?

What do you think causes you to choose that route?

When you have broken trust with your spouse, do you find yourself trying to work your way back into his/her good graces with promises to never fail again? Why is this the wrong approach?

THE BRIGHTNESS OF THE NOON DAY

Seeing our sin and failures is never easy. It's much easier to see the sin in others and to make it our mission to help them see it as well. The Bible has much to say about how light exposes darkness (John 1:5).

The Greek word for **judge not** is translated to "call in question; to separate."[15]

Read what Jesus has to say about seeing our own sin in Matthew 7:1-5.

What was Jesus' reasoning for why we should not judge others?

In verse 3 Jesus asked a question that demands an examination of the heart.

Consider a recent argument with your spouse and ask yourself the two questions Jesus asked here:
1. Why do you easily spot the failure, sin, and flaws in your spouse but don't see your own as clearly?

2. Why is it impossible to help your spouse correct his/ her [failure, sin, flaws] if you haven't submitted your own [failure, sin, flaws] to the Lord?

No one wants to experience having his/her trust broken. But it's also true that we are all guilty of breaking trust.

How might considering Jesus' teaching on examining our own hearts before trying to correct our spouse's lay the groundwork for giving trust?

Trust can never be earned; it must be given. Trust is a gift you give to your spouse over and over. We are hypocrites when we demand to be given trust while simultaneously making others earn it.

In what ways have you withheld the gift of trust from your spouse?

Withholding the gift of trust often says more about our hearts than our spouses'.

In 1 Thessalonians 2:4 Paul stated he was approved by God to be entrusted with the gospel. Paul didn't deserve to be given this level of trust—or any level of trust. In fact, God trusted Paul with the precious gospel of grace when he was on a mission to obliterate all Christians (Acts 9). Yet God called Paul his "chosen instrument" (v. 15).

Christian, you have also been entrusted with the gospel. God has handed to you His ministry of reconciliation—the same ministry that cost His Son His life (2 Cor. 5:18-20).

If God gives us trust, how much more should we give trust to others?

We see a powerful outworking of trust in the relationship of Joseph and Mary staying together and bringing baby Jesus into the world together.

- Joseph and Mary both gave trust to the word of the angel.
- Joseph gave trust to Mary.
- Mary and Joseph's parents gave trust to both Mary and Joseph (culturally implied).
- Mary gave trust to God.

Nothing was easy about what Joseph and Mary did. They must have been terrified. They must have experienced so much cultural shame. We get to read this story without feeling the pain and fear they must have felt. Giving trust in the moment is no easy task. It requires humility, the honesty to see our own sin, the willingness to give others the mercy we have been given, and a total dependence on the help and power of the Holy Spirit.

A PRAYER FOR THE NIGHT

As we said earlier, trust is a gift. Broken trust must be healed for unity to exist. But building trust often takes time. Couples will struggle to move forward if a spouse is refusing to give the precious gift of trust.

Read Proverbs 3:5-8.

What does trusting and fearing the Lord produce in us?

How might placing your trust in the Lord produce in you
a desire to give trust to your spouse?

We are broken, sinful, and flawed people—guaranteed to break one another's
trust. When we are struggling to trust others, the best place to begin
rebuilding trust is by trusting the One who cannot and will not ever hurt us.

Spend a few moments in prayer expressing your trust in God
and asking Him to help you and your spouse build trust in
each other, even when it's hard.

 ## AS YOU GO

Remember this truth: "The steadfast love of the LORD never ceases;
his mercies never come to an end; they are new every morning; great is
your faithfulness. 'The LORD is my portion,' says my soul, 'therefore I will
hope in him'" (Lam. 3:22-24).

Fight for this truth: Giving trust to our spouses requires a deep trust in
the One who will never leave us, forsake us, or fail us.

Pray this truth: *God, thank You for Your Word. Thank You for
teaching me . . .*

Help me to trust and obey You with . . .

Amen

DAY 4

TALK
IT OUT

We encourage you to take a few minutes on this day to sit with your spouse and process what you studied this week. Use some or all of the following questions to guide your discussion:

1. Which day of study was your favorite and why?

2. What was the most difficult portion of the study for you and why?

3. How would you define *submission*?

4. Are you comfortable with this teaching on submission and headship? Why or why not?

5. How do you see our wrong desires overshadowing our desires to love and serve one another?

6. Do we have a healthy way of determining who takes the lead in different situations in our marriage? If so, what are some examples? If not, how can our marriage be stronger in this area?

7. What can we do to be better at offering mercy and grace when we've broken trust with each other?

8. How can I better build trust as your spouse?

9. Which of the "As You Go" statements really captured your heart? Why?

Finish this day by praying together. Take time to list some specific requests you can pray for over each other. Then, spend some time praying about other areas of your marriage that God has revealed to you that need attention or refining.

It's so important that you and your spouse spend quality time together on a consistent basis. You'll need to be purposeful and intentional to make this happen. We want to help. Each week we'll provide one or two simple date night ideas. Of course, "date night" could be a "date morning" or "date afternoon." Whatever best fits your schedule. And if you're wondering what to talk about, feel free to use the designated connection points found throughout this week's study or the discussion questions found on Day 4.

 ## DATE IDEAS FOR THIS WEEK

1. Take a long walk together. Before you leave on your walk, designate the type of conversation you'll have on this walk. For instance, you might take a "dream walk," where the theme of your conversation is about hopes and dreams for the future concerning family, ministry, work, and so forth. Or it could be a "nostalgia walk," where your time is spent recalling cherished moments or special times in your family. Another idea could be a "funny story walk," where you each share funny stories about yourself or embarrassing moments you've experienced.

2. Build a fire together and have a fireside chat. This could happen in front of your fireplace at home, around a fire pit on your patio, or around a fire you build on your property or friends' property (with their permission, of course). Wherever your fire, pull up chairs, relax, and talk about the history of your love together. Talk about first falling in love but also discuss moments when the fire of your love dimmed in your relationship. You might even talk about how you can heat things up romantically in your marriage.

FIGHTING AND FORGIVING

#COMPLEMENTSTUDY

I sat on one side of the room; he sat on the other. We were exhausted from fighting with no resolution. For days we avoided one another in a thick silence. But nothing was peaceful about our quiet house. Both of us were immovable. Both of us thought we were right. Both of us had strong points. What now?

> *THE CYCLE OF FIGHTING AND FORGIVING IS A NECESSARY PART OF MARRIAGE.*

This kind of fighting was my greatest fear about marriage. What do you do when you just can't come to a solution? How do you keep loving the person who hurt you? Do you just get over it? Do you just give in?

The cycle of fighting and forgiving is a necessary part of marriage. In fact, it might be the very thing that helps you learn and understand more about your spouse. Fighting reveals our desires. Have you ever been in a fight with your spouse, and, as he/she was making his/her points, you thought—*Wait. I had no idea he/she even cared about this sort of thing.* Or, in the midst of a standoff, you realized you were holding onto something so tightly that you had alienated your spouse's feelings?

It's easy to believe that if we could just stop fighting, our marriage would be better. But the truth is, when fighting is done well, it can be the very thing that grows and deepens your relationship. It is not the fighting that needs

111

to end; it's the way we fight that must mature. For a relationship to benefit from conflict, the posture of both spouses must be: *I'm fighting for you, not against you.*

To be for our spouses means that regardless of what is revealed in a fight, we are committed to loving, caring, and forgiving our spouses the way Christ loves, cares, and forgives us. This week we will learn about how to fight and forgive in a way that honors God and one another.

NOTES

REVIEW

1. Which day of study was the most meaningful to you? Why?

2. What does it mean to *submit*? What does it mean for a wife to submit to her husband? For both spouses to mutually submit to each other?

3. How does mutual submission produce freedom in a marriage?

4. What happens when your selfish desires overwhelm your desire to love and serve your spouse? How can you keep that from happening?

5. Do you agree that husbands and wives are both called to lead in different ways and in different times? Explain.

6. Do you and your spouse pray for each other? Do you pray with each other? Why are both needed?

7. What are some recent new mercies God has blessed you with? How does seeing your spouse as a new mercy from the Lord affect your view of him/her?

8. What are some things that can decrease the trust level in your marriage? What can you do to increase that level?

9. Did you do one of the Date Night ideas? If so, share about your experience.

WATCH THE VIDEO

DISCUSS

1. What part of the video really got your attention? Why?

2. Do you and your spouse fight well? Explain.

3. Do you think it is possible for conflict in your marriage to be a good thing? How?

4. What fuels your fights?

5. What does it mean to fight for your spouse instead of against your spouse in the middle of conflict? What makes that difficult to do?

6. Which are you better at, fighting or forgiving? Explain.

7. Why is asking for and granting forgiveness so hard at times?

8. Do you and your spouse handle conflict better now than you did when you first got married? Explain.

DAY

FIGHTING WITH THE END IN MIND

Father,
Show us what a redeemed version of our marriage looks like. Help us to love one another, to fight for one another, and to treat one another in a way that reflects the greater and eternal marriage between Christ and the church.
Amen

The end goal of marital conflict should always be unity. When we engage in a conflict with restoration as the end goal, it changes the landscape of the fight. Imagine you are going on a road trip. If you don't know your destination and you make turns based on a gut feeling, to escape traffic, or for whatever reason, chances are you will drive in circles and wear yourself out without ever getting anywhere. But if you know where you're headed, you're more likely to stay on course and not get distracted.

Fighting with the end in mind holds the same principle. If our destination is restoration, it changes the way we fight. Jesus cares deeply about the unity of the church and unity in our marriages. Remember—our marriages reflect the unbreakable love of God for the church. When conflict happens, and it will, we are called to forgive, reconcile, and seek full restoration and unity.

Read Ephesians 5:25-31.

What do you imagine a church that is splendidly holy—without spot, wrinkle, or blemish—to look like? How do you imagine the people of that church would treat one another?

Continue that ideation: What do you imagine a marriage that is representing a splendidly holy church to look like? How do you imagine the husband and wife would treat one another?

Think back to when you and your spouse first knew you would get married. What did you imagine your marriage would be like? Write down everything you thought it would be.

This exercise is not intended to highlight unmet expectations in your marriage. However, it's likely that those imaginings were unfettered by differing opinions, goals, and preferences. When conflict enters a relationship, it becomes important to remember the desired end goal. Knowing what we want our marriage to represent creates standards for how we will treat one another when things are difficult.

WHAT IS THE END GOAL OF CONFLICT?
Read John 17:22-23.

Jesus prayed that His children would be one just like God the Father, God the Son, and God the Spirit are one. Why did Jesus ask His Father to produce this deep unity?

CONNECTION POINT

Discuss your answers to these questions together.

How might reminding one another of the end goal help create healthy boundaries in an argument?

....

....

One way to engage in healthy conflict is to start the conversation with the end goal. We have provided a conflict starter below. Using the example, write your own version of a conflict starter to remind you and your spouse of the end goal of a conflict.

We need to talk about _____, but what I want you to hear from me and fight to keep in mind is that I love you, and I am for us.

....

....

....

Now we all know that sometimes, maybe most of the time, fights just erupt. And before we've had time to talk about the end goal, harsh and hurtful words have been spoken. In those moments, the first person you have to remind about the end goal is yourself. So take a step back and remember you're not fighting against each other. Then, move forward to solve the conflict.

RECOGNIZE YOUR SIN.

To fight with the end in mind, we must keep the beginning in mind. Pride is at the root of all sin. We are not so unlike Adam and Eve believing we can find a better, more satisfying freedom apart from God. The sin of pride shows up in all of our fights. It's what slows down forgiveness.

C. S. Lewis said this about the sin of pride:

> There is one vice of which no man in the world is free;
> which everyone in the world loathes when he sees
> it in someone else; and of which hardly any people,
> except Christians, ever imagine that they are guilty
> themselves. . . . There is no fault which makes a man
> more unpopular, and no fault which we are more
> unconscious of in ourselves. And the more we have it
> ourselves, the more we dislike it in others. . . . Pride
> leads to every other vice: it is the complete anti-God
> state of mind.[1]

Read the following verses. In each verse, what does pride cause?

SCRIPTURE	WHAT PRIDE CAUSES
In his pride the wicked man does not seek him; in all his thoughts there is no room for God (Ps. 10:4, NIV).	
Where there is strife, there is pride, but wisdom is found in those who take advice (Prov. 13:10, NIV).	
Pride goes before destruction, a haughty spirit before a fall (Prov. 16:18, NIV).	

With an ongoing conflict in mind, answer the following questions:

What is ruling my heart—pride or humility?

Am I fighting for or against my spouse?

REPENTANCE

Sometimes we think acknowledging our sin brings change instantly, but recognizing our sin is only the first part of the process. Largely due to our authenticity culture, many of us will readily talk about how much of a hot mess we are. Unlike the generations that have gone before us, we're fairly comfortable recognizing and even confessing our sins—perhaps even becoming part of popular culture. But repentance does not come so easily because repentance means changing one's behavior.

Eugene Peterson described true repentance like this:

> *Repentance is not an emotion. It is not feeling sorry for your sins. . . . Repentance is a realization that what God wants from you and what you want from God are not going to be achieved by doing the same old things, thinking the same old thoughts. Repentance is a decision to follow Jesus Christ and become his pilgrim in the path of peace.*[2]

Read Romans 2:4.

Where does the desire to repent come from?

How does God's kindness lead you to repentance? How have you experienced this?

Read 2 Corinthians 7:10.

What is the difference between godly grief and worldly grief?

What does godly grief produce that worldly grief does not?

It is difficult to tell the difference between the feeling of godly grief and worldly grief. Both might cause us to feel bad, sad, or ashamed. But Scripture says we can tell which type of grief we are operating out of based on what it compels us to do. Godly grief will compel us to seek forgiveness and full redemption from Jesus. Godly grief is swallowed up by the grace and mercy of the cross. Worldly grief will compel us to try and fix the problem ourselves or just wait it out until enough time has passed to make us feel less sensitive to it.

Is God bringing any sin to mind that you need to repent of? Take a moment and ask God to forgive you. Ask Him to set you on the path of peace.

Repentance has two necessary parts—repentance before God and repentance before others.

REPENT BEFORE GOD.

Read Mark 1:15.

What was the call to action in Jesus' preaching?

Read Acts 2:37-38; 3:19-20.

What was the call to action in the apostles' preaching?

From early in the ministry of Jesus and early in the apostles' ministry, the call was for the people to repent of their sins and believe. When Peter preached on the day of Pentecost, the Scriptures state that the people were "cut to the heart" and desperately cried out "what shall we do?" (Acts 2:37). Peter's immediate response: "Repent" (v. 38). They were to change their minds and hearts by faith about who they were and what they'd done and to trust in who Jesus was and what He'd done. It's the same for us. We no longer trust in ourselves and our own righteousness, but now we trust in Jesus and His work on the cross. There is no salvation apart from this.

REPENT BEFORE ONE ANOTHER.

We are to carry this attitude of repentance into solving our conflicts with each other. We must be willing to realize how we've wronged each other, confess that sin, ask for forgiveness, and change our behavior toward each other.

Is there a wrong you need to repent of and seek forgiveness for with your spouse? If so, take immediate action. Walk to where your spouse is, make a phone call, send a text, or write a note to begin the process of making things right with your spouse.

RELINQUISH YOUR RIGHTS.

Rights, by definition, are what we are justly entitled to. If we have a justified claim to our rights, why would we ever knowingly and willingly give them up? The not-so-Sunday-School answer: *Jesus*. Jesus relinquished His rights to the power and comfort of heaven to pursue us in love (Phil. 2:7). We are called to imitate Him by relinquishing our own rights in order to love others as He has loved us.

Dr. Tony Evans said,

> *When Jesus Christ did something about your sin and mine, He didn't give us the leftovers. He poured all that made Him God into man so that man would have all of God. There is nothing that belonged to God that man didn't have when Jesus emptied Himself into man.*[3]

Truly relinquishing our rights does not mean we just give up extra privileges; it means laying down our very lives (Mark 8:34-35).

We all have certain things that are precious to us, making them difficult to give up for the sake of our spouses. What are some things that are difficult to lay down in order to love your spouse well? Be specific.

CONNECTION POINT

Discuss your answers to these questions together.

Take an honest look at your marital conflict. How have you seen it weaken your marriage? Strengthen it?

....

....

....

....

....

How can you approach marital conflict keeping the end in mind—aiming for unity and fighting for your spouse—instead of just unloading frustration, anger, or unmet preferences on your spouse?

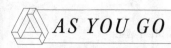

AS YOU GO

Remember this truth: "Think of yourselves the way Christ Jesus thought of himself. He had equal status with God but didn't think so much of himself that he had to cling to the advantages of that status no matter what. Not at all. When the time came, he set aside the privileges of deity and took on the status of a slave, became *human*! Having become human, he stayed human. It was an incredibly humbling process. He didn't claim special privileges. Instead, he lived a selfless, obedient life and then died a selfless, obedient death—and the worst kind of death at that—a crucifixion" (Phil. 2:5-8, The Message).

Fight for this truth: Fighting with the end in mind—unity with your spouse—sets you on a path of peace and creates beneficial boundaries that help you fight for one another instead of against one another.

Pray this truth: *God, thank You for Your Word. Thank You for teaching me . . .*

Help me to trust and obey You with . . .

Amen

DAY

2

FIGHTING + FORGIVING

Father,
Help me to acknowledge that while I was still Your enemy You pursued me, loved me, died for me, and rose again for me. You didn't just say You wanted to be united to me; everything You did was an action of unity. Help me to follow Your example of pursuing unity at all costs in my marriage.
Amen

THE ART OF FIGHTING WELL

Many couples believe the goal of a happy marriage is to be conflict free. That might be a possible goal to achieve during the time of dating, engagement, and early marriage. But the reality is that a fight is coming, and it might be the very best thing for your marriage. Healthy conflict demands a level of trust that we aren't willing to give to just anyone. It takes guts to choose healthy conflict with your spouse.

CONNECTION POINT

Discuss your answer to this question together.

In what ways does believing your relationship will be conflict-free create false expectations for your marriage?

Every family deals with conflict a little differently. Consider
how your parents dealt with it when you were growing up. How
did the way they approached conflict shape the way you view
it today?

CONNECTION POINT

Discuss
your
answers
to these
questions
together.

How did your family's fighting style differ from your spouse's? What
are some healthy ways to deal with conflict that you've learned
from both families? What are some of the unhealthy ways you've
seen that you want to drop?

....

....

....

Most of us fall into one of three broad categories when it comes to how we
handle conflict.

Choose the one below you think is your primary style.
Complete the final sentence to express why.

AVOIDANCE	AGGRESSION	ACCOMODATION
Avoidance believes the lie that refusing to engage in conflict is healthier. This is often propped up by believing that the best and happiest marriages are the conflict-free marriages.	Aggression believes the lie that it is best to engage in conflict without restraint. This is often propped up by believing that your authenticity is more important than the other person.	Accomodation believes the lie that as long as a semblance of "peace" is in the home, things are fine. This is often built on a wrong understanding of peace. Compromise for self-preservation often leads to the couple not really knowing one another.

AVOIDANCE	AGGRESSION	ACCOMODATION
I tend to avoid conflict because I believe . . .	I tend to be the aggressor in conflict because I believe . . .	I tend to accommodate for the sake of peace because I believe . . .

Fighting in marriage is bound to happen at some point. Setting up an impossible goal to never fight is unrealistic and unhealthy. Today, we are going to focus on practical ways to have healthy conflict.

KNOW WHY YOU'RE FIGHTING.

Read James 4:1.

Why do we fight?

The Book of James says our passions, or desires for pleasure, cause conflict among us. Think of your own marriage. Is this true of you?

Identifying our passions is step one in fighting well. Most of us are willing to defend and fight for the things we want. James 4:2a says,

> *You desire and do not have, so you murder. You covet and cannot obtain, so you fight and quarrel.*

CONNECTION POINT

Discuss your answers to these questions together.

What are the passions and desires you're willing to fight about to protect, defend, or obtain? We have provided a few categories these passions and desires might fit in but feel free to add your own categories and examples.

Preferences

(Example: I function better in a clean and organized home. It's worth hurting my spouse's feelings if it results in a cleaner home.)

What do your preferences reveal about your heart?

....

....

....

Expectations

(Example: I expect my spouse to _____. If he/she doesn't do this, it communicates to me a lack of consideration or love.)

What do your expectations reveal about your heart?

....

....

....

Priorities

(Example: I think _____ is something we should be focused on in our marriage. If my spouse really cared, he/she would see it that way also.)

What do your priorities reveal about your heart?

....

....

....

RULES OF ENGAGEMENT

Imagine this scenario: Bob comes home, and the house is a wreck. He doesn't say anything, but when Sally tries to give him a kiss, she can feel the distance and tension in his body. "You okay?" she asks. He grunts back, "Yeah, I'm fine." Two hours later he watches her step over a kid's toy to go to another room, and it sets him off. "Can't you just pick it up?" he snaps at her. And the fight is on. He's frustrated. She's angry and hurt. This is not the time to attempt to draw boundaries for a fight.

SOME WORDS ARE OFF-LIMITS.

Read Proverbs 12:18.

CONNECTION POINT

Discuss your answer to this question together.

What metaphor did the poet use to describe hurtful words?

....
....
....
....
....

What specific words are deeply hurtful for you? Write them in the space on the next page and tell why they cut you like a sword. (Consider: curse words, blaming words, name-calling, words that identified you pre-Jesus, etc.) For example: My husband and I have never really used "pet names" for one another. So, when we fight and he uses words like "sweetheart," it feels condescending and sends me to next-level anger. So, my answer might look like this:

Words that are off-limits	Why?
"Sweetheart"	I feel like you're hiding a host of meanness by using a kind word spitefully. I feel condescended and manipulated.

Words that are off-limits	Why?

Knowing what words hurt your spouse and not using them are a way to communicate value and care. But sharing this with your spouse requires a deep level of trust. Don't use this information as a weapon but as a way to strengthen your marriage.

SOME ACTIONS ARE OFF-LIMITS.

CONNECTION POINT

Discuss this verse together.

Read Proverbs 15:18.

....

....

....

In the heat of conflict, we are all tempted to emphasize our point, our hurt, or our feelings in different ways.

What are some unhealthy actions you use to drive your perspective home? (Consider: walking away, throwing things, taking wedding ring off, refusing to look the other person in the eyes, manipulating through tears, etc.) For example: When I am really angry and want to hurt my spouse, I take my wedding ring off and slam it down before I walk away.

What hurtful actions need to be off-limits?

KNOW WHEN TO TAKE A BREAK.

Read *Proverbs 17:14.*

The *ESV Study Bible* explains the proverb like this:

> *Once a dam has been breached, there is no holding back the water—an apt image for the rapid and damaging escalation of a quarrel.*[4]

Consider together some phrases you and your spouse have said but need to wisely avoid to keep the fighting from escalating. For example: *I need a minute. I'm not leaving you, and I'm not going anywhere, but let's come back to this in (X-amount of time). I want to talk about this, but if we keep at this now I'm going to say something I regret. Can we come back to this in (X-amount of time)?*

CONNECTION POINT

Discuss your answer to this question together.

When I need to take a break, I will say:

....

....

....

....

....

Notice that in each of these examples, there is a set time to come back together. This lowers the risk of just moving on without resolving the conflict. Understand that burying the conflict is dangerous for the long-term health of your relationship. It is unloving to refuse to work through conflict.

HOW TO TALK ABOUT YOUR SPOUSE IN FRONT OF OTHERS.

We've all been in one of those awkward moments when a husband or wife throws his/her spouse under the bus for the sake of a laugh or lets some residual anger from an unresolved fight slip out. It's critical you establish boundaries for how and when you talk about your spouse in front of others.

CONNECTION POINT

Discuss your answer to this question together.

It hurts my feelings when you say/do this in front of other people:

....

....

....

....

....

....

THE ART OF FORGIVING WELL

Part of fighting well is forgiving fully. Let's see what the Word says about how to forgive one another the way God in Christ forgave us.

WHY DO WE FORGIVE?
Read Ephesians 4:32.

What reason did Paul give for why we should forgive others?

He wrote, be "compassionate" (CSB) or be "tenderhearted" (v. 32). Maintaining a posture of tenderness in an argument requires dependence on the Holy Spirit.

HOW OFTEN DO WE FORGIVE?
Read Matthew 18:21-35 and rewrite the parable in your own words.

What does Jesus desire us to understand from this parable (v. 33)?

Consider a recent conflict or tension in your marriage. What would it look like to apply the kind of mercy and forgiveness this parable teaches?

Are there particular wounds or wrongs your spouse has committed against you that are more difficult for you to forgive? What makes them more difficult?

LOVE KEEPS NO RECORD OF WRONGS

The first week of our study, we read the "love chapter"—1 Corinthians 13. In this chapter, Paul gave some great advice when it comes to maintaining a posture of love and forgiveness in marriage. He said love, "Doesn't keep score of the sins of others . . ." (1 Cor. 13:3-7, The Message).

Why do you believe Paul insisted that loving other people means not keeping a scorecard of ways they have sinned or wronged you? What might keeping a scorecard reveal about your heart?

Imagine a situation in which every time you had a fight with your spouse, you had no memory or recollection of past ways he/she hurt you. Think how less intense the fight would be. How much quicker you would forgive. This is essentially what Paul was counseling Christians to do. While it may never be possible to forget how you've been wronged, you can intentionally choose to never hold it over that person. To keep no record of that wrong. How do we do that?

Read Psalm 103:12 and Hebrews 8:12 and write down what God chooses to do with our sin against Him.

CONNECTION POINT

Spend time praying over this together.

The depth of God's gift of forgiveness toward us is what we are to model in our relationship with our spouses. Spend some time praying and processing with your spouse ways that you want to grow in the art of fighting and forgiving well.

AS YOU GO

Remember this truth: "He has removed our sins as far from us as the east is from the west" (Ps. 103:12, NLT).

Fight for this truth: We, as Christians, are called to be tenderhearted and kind, forgiving fully as Christ forgave us.

Pray this truth: God, thank You for Your Word. Thank You for teaching me . . .

Help me to trust and obey You with . . .

Amen

3

HEALING
FORWARD

Father,
Help me to surrender my shame and my wounds to You. Help me to believe that You can and want to heal the parts of me that hurt the most. Teach me to be a tender, loving, and kind spouse that reflects the way You have poured out Your tender mercies on me.
Amen

Kintsugi, or *golden joinery*, is the ancient Japanese art of repairing broken pottery into a masterful new piece. Rather than hiding the fractures or discarding the piece as unusable, the potter highlights the imperfections with gold, silver, and platinum powders.[5] We, too, are broken and imperfect vessels. But God is a kind Artisan. He promises to take what is old, unusable, and broken and transform us into new creations. God redeems and restores all of our brokenness into beauty.

In our marriages, when we wound our spouses with our words, our sin, our selfishness, God commands us to extend the same gift of forgiveness that He has extended to us. But what happens when our sin has broken our marriages into seemingly unfixable pieces? The answer, though stunningly beautiful, is not easy. Jesus not only forgave us, but He reconciled and restored us. The greatest illustration of reconciliation is the cross of Christ.

We must consider three things when working through reconciliation in our marriages. 1) Remember reconciliation to seek reconciliation. 2) Reconciliation should not be punitive. 3) Reconciliation takes time.

1. REMEMBER RECONCILIATION TO SEEK RECONCILIATION.

> *Reconciliation comes from the Greek family of words that has its roots in allasso [ἀλλάσσο]. The meaning common to this word group is "change" or "exchange." Reconciliation involves a change in the relationship between God and man or man and man. It assumes there has been a breakdown in the relationship, but now there has been a change from a state of enmity and fragmentation to one of harmony and fellowship.[6]*

Read Romans 5:1-11. In the image below, underneath the word *BROKEN*, list the four words (ESV) used to describe a person pre-Christ. Then, read 2 Corinthians 5:14-21 and, underneath *MINISTRY OF RECONCILIATION*, write down verses 18 and 19.

RECONCILED

BROKEN   PEACE WITH GOD   MINISTRY OF
          THROUGH CHRIST   RECONCILIATION

Reflecting on who we were before Christ—weak, ungodly, sinful enemies—reminds us of the darkness Christ pulled us out of. He purchased us by the blood of His love so we can live in the light of His love. We have been rescued, reconciled, and redeemed. Because the darkness has no power over us, we can stare it straight in the eye and be reminded of the powerful mercy and grace of Jesus.

Theologian and pastor Charles Spurgeon wrote,

> *That was our character. There was no good point*
> *about us. We were ungodly and we had no strength*
> *to mend ourselves or to be other than ungodly. The*
> *strength for reformation had all gone. The strength*
> *for regeneration we never had. We were without*
> *strength, and then Christ died for us—died for the*
> *ungodly. . . . And that is the glory of his love. While*
> *we were rebels against his government, he redeemed*
> *us. While we were far off from him by wicked works*
> *he sent his Son to die and bring us near. Free grace,*
> *indeed, was this—not caused by anything in us, but*
> *springing freely from the great heart of God.*[7]

Take a few moments to reflect on the unfathomable love, grace, and mercy Jesus poured out on you so that you could have peace with God. Write a few words of praise and thanksgiving for the power of the cross in your life.

Reconciliation can be described as "making it right."

What comes to mind when you hear this term?

Consider a Christian's call to be a minister of reconciliation. How do you think this applies to the marriage relationship?

God chose His children when we were weak, ungodly, and sinful enemies. We had no way of earning our salvation or strategizing our rescue. We were utterly hopeless. The exact thing we needed was the exact gift God gave us. We needed a way to stand before a holy God, so God made a way—at a great cost to Himself. Jesus became our sin so we could stand on and in His righteousness. Remembering this great exchange and reflecting this kind of mercy, love, and grace is how we experience healing and reconciliation in our marriages. When our spouses sin against us—we remember how often we sin against God. When our spouses do something hurtful—we remember that we, too, are capable of hurting them. Even when our spouses reject or betray us—we remember God chose to give up His Son for us while we were rejecting and rebelling against Him. Christ's reconciliation is the foundation and example for how we treat our spouses when they wrong us.

2. RECONCILIATION SHOULD NOT BE PUNITIVE.

Seeking healing and reconciliation in a marriage can feel complicated for believers. We wrestle with questions like—*Am I supposed to just get over it? What do I do with all my anger and hurt feelings? Are there no consequences for wrongdoing?*

We need to remember how God treats us in our sin. He doesn't let sin slide, but by grace, He washes us clean and forgives every sin. And even after we come to know Him, if we stray, He lovingly disciplines us—to restore us, not to punish us (Heb. 12:5-11).

How is a desire to punish your spouse for hurting you not reflective of the heart of God?

What might it look like to fight the desire to punish your spouse and instead slowly move toward restoration?

Read Genesis 50:15-21.

Joseph's brothers knew their past treatment of Joseph was an inconceivable evil. Even though Joseph had already expressed forgiveness toward them (Gen. 45:1-15), they assumed it wouldn't stick, especially since their father was now dead.

> What did Joseph's brothers fear Joseph would want to do? In what ways has a fear of retaliation hindered you from acknowledging wrongdoing and asking forgiveness from someone you hurt?

> What was Joseph's response to his brothers? (See Gen. 50:19.)

> What did Joseph mean when he said that God meant the brothers' evil for good? What was the good that came from Joseph's suffering?

Joseph walked through a painful experience. But God was sovereign and redeemed all of it for His purpose. We expect the people closest to us to treat us with loyalty and love. But that doesn't always happen. God's mercy and forgiveness doesn't ignore the crushing pain of betrayal. Scripture talks about pain and suffering in depth, telling us it's going to happen. God gives meaning to our suffering, creates a path for healing, and promises us that one day we will be completely whole—not one cell of our body will have a trace of brokenness in it. Not one memory will hold the pain we feel now.

Consider the way Joseph forgave, reconciled with his brothers, and fully restored a relationship with them. Pray, asking God to show you how to reconcile and restore like Joseph and his brothers.

3. RECONCILIATION TAKES TIME.

Imagine this scenario: a wife betrays her husband's confidence by reconnecting with an old boyfriend. The relationship felt benign at first, but as they caught up, her feelings were reignited. Realizing she was wrong, she ended the conversation, removed the social media site from her phone, and confessed to her husband. He was obviously wounded by her actions. He was gracious to forgive, but then over the next few weeks he continued to act coldly toward his wife. This frustrated her to the point that she snapped at him—*Get over it already! I apologized. I ended it. You're acting like a baby.*

What went wrong here? Confession happened. Forgiveness happened. But still, they were unable to find their way back to the peace and trust they once had.

Read Amos 9:11-15 to learn what restoration looked like for Israel.

In verse 11 (ESV), God said He would:

_____ its breaches (gaps or broken places);

_____ _____ its ruins;

_____ it (Israel) as in the days of old.

Each of these restorative actions takes time. It takes time to rebuild trust that has been broken.

Think about a recent argument you had with your spouse.
Using that argument as a framework, work through the
following steps of reconciliation:

TAKE RESPONSIBILITY.

True repentance owns the sin committed. We can fully own what we did
wrong because Jesus fully paid the price for it.

In your argument, did you fully own your part of the problem?
Why or why not? What kept you from fully owning your part?

PRAY.

Psalm 34:18 promises that God will be near the brokenhearted. One way,
arguably the most important way, to pursue reconciliation is to ask the Lord
to heal what's been broken.

In your argument, did you spend time praying for the Lord to
bring healing? Why or why not? How did you see God answer
your prayers to soften one another's hearts and move you
toward reconciliation?

EXERCISE PATIENCE.

Patience is a fruit of the Spirit (Gal. 5:22). We must pray and ask God
to help us to be patient as the Lord heals the wounds we have caused
our spouses.

In your argument, did you find yourself getting frustrated that
your spouse was taking too long to heal? What does your
impatience reveal to you about your heart?

EMPATHIZE.

Feelings are real. Oftentimes, forgiveness has been granted, but feelings are still hurt. One way to heal forward is by empathizing with your spouse's wounded feelings. Give space for him/her to feel how he/she feels and trust the Lord to heal.

> In your argument, did you judge your spouse for not having godly feelings? What might it look like to empathize with your spouse's hurt or wounded feelings while not encouraging him/her to sit in sin?

PURSUE.

Just like God pursues us, we must be intentional in slowly and tenderly inviting our spouses back into relationship activities that will produce trust and friendship.

> As you were reconciling with your spouse, did you take the posture of humility to pursue your spouse? If your spouse was not quite ready to step into that level of trust, how did you process the rejection?

ENCOURAGE.

As you see your spouse taking difficult steps of faith, healing, and trust, encourage him/her in what you see the Lord doing. We all know how difficult it can be to take a step of faith when trust has been broken. Take the opportunity to share with your spouse how you see God moving in his/her life.

As you were reconciling, did you speak words of encouragement? Did your words show your spouse that you are in this with him/her? Why or why not? How can you encourage your spouse when he/she is working through difficult emotions?

If you and your spouse are in a season of reconciliation, consider ways that you can pray, pursue, and praise one another. Write a letter to your spouse using the preceding reconciliatory steps.

If you and your spouse are not in a season of reconciliation, spend time processing how you might handle broken trust and broken hearts in the future.

AS YOU GO

Remember this truth: "For while we were still weak, at the right time Christ died for the ungodly. For one will scarcely die for a righteous person—though perhaps for a good person one would dare even to die—but God shows his love for us in that while we were still sinners, Christ died for us" (Rom. 5:6-8).

Fight for this truth: God reconciling us to Himself through Christ is the foundation and example of how we are to treat our spouses when they wrong us.

Pray this truth: *God, thank You for Your Word. Thank You for teaching me . . .*

Help me to trust and obey You with . . .

Amen

DAY

TALK
IT OUT

We encourage you to take a few minutes on this day to sit with your spouse and process what you studied this week. Use some or all of the following questions to guide your discussion:

1. Which day of study was your favorite and why?

2. What was the most difficult portion of the study for you and why?

3. How have we let pride cause conflict in our marriage? How can we choose humility instead?

4. Do you think we do a good job of forgiving one another? Why or why not? How can we get better at this?

5. What's the silliest argument we've ever had? What can we do to not let minor things become huge sources of conflict?

6. What are some boundaries we need to draw for our fights? What words or actions are off-limits?

7. Do you ever feel like you're trying to deal with conflict in our marriage by yourself? If so, why? What can I do to change that?

8. How have we seen God take the difficult, broken times in our marriage and use them for good and His purpose?

9. Which of the "As You Go" statements really captured your heart? Why?

Finish this day by praying together. Take time to list some specific requests you can pray for over each other. Then, spend some time praying about other areas of your marriage God has revealed to you that need attention or refining.

It's so important that you and your spouse spend quality time together on a consistent basis. You'll need to be purposeful and intentional to make this happen. We want to help. Each week we'll provide one or two simple date night ideas. Of course, "date night" could be a "date morning" or "date afternoon." Whatever best fits your schedule. And if you're wondering what to talk about, feel free to use the designated connection points found throughout this week's study or the discussion questions found on Day 4.

 ## DATE IDEAS FOR THIS WEEK

1. Spend your date night this week serving together. Here are some ideas: Volunteer at a homeless shelter or a nursing home. Prepare food together for a family in crisis and take it to them. Spend time with some senior adults in your church who may find it difficult to get out and about. Find out the needs of single parents in your church or neighborhood and do what you can to meet those needs. We're sure there are tons of other ideas. However you choose to serve, just do it together with hearts of humility.

2. Take a mini road trip together. Check out the cities and towns within an hour's drive from where you live. Find something interesting and unique to go do or see in one of those neighboring towns. Take a picnic lunch with you or choose a restaurant that seems to be a favorite of the locals.

SE/X

#COMPLEMENTSTUDY

Our view of sex creates our expectations about sex. If you were raised in church in the '80s and '90s, you might resonate with the following experience: *Hundreds of kids are sitting in an auditorium listening to a goatee-d youth pastor teach on the importance of sexual purity. As he speaks, an older volunteer hands*

> IF YOU AND YOUR SPOUSE HAVE STRUGGLED WITH SEX IN YOUR MARRIAGE, YOU ARE NOT ALONE.

a single white rose to a student on the front row, whispering, "Pass it down." The white rose passes through the hands of each teenager, only to arrive broken and wilted at the last row. The volunteer then brings the rose up to the stage and hands it over to the youth pastor on cue to dramatically end his talk. As the youth pastor holds up the remains of the tarnished rose, he says, "And this is what you will be like if you give away your virginity. Is this really what you want to give your husband or wife on the night of your wedding?" And then lots of kids, some terrified, some resolute, signed a contract to maintain their virginity.

Perhaps you didn't experience the church's somewhat misguided, bland, or often silent approach to the topic, rather you looked to culture to teach you about sex. From a few TV shows, a couple of movies, and a pop song or two, you might have determined God had nothing to do with "good" sex. The cultural narrative teaches that sex is power—just make sure you end up on the right side of the equation. Words like *God, marriage,* and *covenant* are sex-killers instead of sex-thrillers. These cultural influences teach that on-call rooms, club bathrooms, and the back of cars with a parade of non-spouses guarantee better sex than any loving, God-honoring marriage ever could. The message is loud and clear—sex within the bounds of marriage is boring and infrequent.

Whether you waited until your wedding day to experience your first kiss or gave in to every sexual urge before saying "I do," every spouse has an expectation of what sex will be like or an idea of what he/she wants it to be. Maybe you imagined that marriage would be a nonstop sexcapade. Maybe you dreamed of how your husband would pursue you perfectly with the right amounts of romance, play, and passion. Maybe your past experiences with sex are full of dark, scary, or sorrowful shadows. Maybe you believed that because you were faithful to say no before marriage, you were guaranteed a lifetime of nonstop orgasms.

If you and your spouse have struggled with sex in your marriage, you are not alone. Many couples feel like their marriage suffocates under failed sexual expectations but don't know whether they should attempt to kill the expectation or find someone else who can meet them. Couples sense their unrealistic expectations are fracturing their unity and intimacy but don't know how to stop it. They silently grapple with the guilt of expectations being set too high and the frustration that sex by God's rules means setting their expectations too low.

Any of this sound familiar?

This week we are going to learn what God—the Creator of sex—thinks about sex. We will see that Scripture is not quiet about how precious, powerful, and pleasurable sex is intended to be within the confines of marriage. Our prayer for you is that as you and your spouse work through this study, God will inspire you by His Word to see and believe that no sex is as amazing as sex the way God intended it to be.

NOTES

REVIEW

1. Which day of study was the most meaningful to you? Why?

2. Are you more likely to relish conflict or avoid it? Explain.

3. What does it mean to fight for each other instead of against each other?

4. How can conflict actually strengthen a marriage?

5. Why do some words need to be off-limits when you're fighting?

6. Why is the way we talk about our spouses in front of people such a huge issue?

7. What seem to be the biggest hindrances to forgiveness in your marriage relationship?

8. What are some keys for reconciliation to take place after trust has been broken in a marriage?

9. Did you do one of the Date Night ideas? If so, share about your experience.

WATCH THE VIDEO

DISCUSS

1. What part of the video really got your attention? Why?

2. How has culture distorted God's good design for sex?

3. Does this topic make you uncomfortable? Why or why not?

4. What were you taught about sex growing up? How did that shape your view of it? How is it still shaping you?

5. Do you think the church has done a good job of helping us understand God's design for sex? If so, how? If not, why not?

6. Have you ever struggled with the lie that the shame of your past is greater than the redemption of your future? Explain.

7. Aaron and Jamie say we all come into marriage with sexual brokenness. Do you agree with that statement? Explain.

8. How can you move past your sexual brokenness in order to have a flourishing and fun sex life with your spouse?

DAY

GOD'S GOOD DESIGN FOR SEX

Father,
Your Word says all good things come from You. Sometimes sex feels like it belongs more to the world than to You. Help me to see You as the mastermind behind the beauty and purpose of sex and as the Redeemer of all the ways sin has broken and distorted sex.
Amen

As with everything else God does, God created sex to reveal His good and inexhaustible love for the world. In our fallen state, we have distorted and minimized sex to be primarily about our base nature of "getting." But God had so much more in mind when He designed sex. Let's look at some of the purposes of sex in marriage.

ONE FLESH

When you marry, you take on a new identity of oneness. Then, you spend the rest of your marriage learning how to develop this oneness so you can enjoy the passion, friendship, and partnership marriage is meant to be. But, as you might have discovered, developing a deep and meaningful oneness can be a difficult and complicated process. Two sinners, two genders, two life stories, two sexual histories, two sets of expectations, two sets of needs and wants, and two personalities—become one person.

Marital oneness is more than sex, but it is not less. On the day of your marriage ceremony, you committed your entire person to your spouse. In the eyes of God, you became a new family, a married entity, unable to be torn apart.

Read Genesis 2:24.

From whom is the man separating and to whom is the man supposed to hold fast?

The Scripture says they "become one flesh" (v. 24). What do you think that means?

> *In the Bible, the word flesh doesn't simply mean your body. It doesn't simply mean what the English word flesh means, which always means simply skin, sinew, blood, and guts. Actually, there's a place in the Bible where God says, "I will pour out my Spirit upon all flesh . . ." That doesn't mean, "I will pour out my Spirit on everybody's body." It means, "I'll pour out my Spirit on all people." The word flesh means a person. When it says the two will become one flesh, it says you'll be one person.*
>
> *You're really no longer the same two people, but you're a third entity. This oneness is tremendously deep. It's organic. It's vital. It's not mechanical.[1]*
>
> *One flesh refers to the personal union of a man and woman at all levels of their lives.[2]*
> **DR. TIMOTHY KELLER**

What do you think the concept of "one flesh" (v. 24) in marriage reveals about God?

How does sex in marriage promote oneness?

NAKED + UNASHAMED

God designed sex to be a sacred experience between a husband and wife.

Read Genesis 2:25.

> What destructive emotion did the husband and wife not experience while they were naked together?

What is shame?

"Shame is a painful emotion that responds to a sense of failure to attain some ideal state. Shame encompasses the entire self. . . . The physical expressions of shame include the blushing face, slumped head, and averted eyes. It generates a wish to hide, to disappear, or even to die."[3]

Nakedness—physically and spiritually—was intended to promote unity between a husband and a wife. Yet, we'll see that when Adam and Eve sinned, they saw their nakedness in a way God never intended for them to see it—as something that could produce shame and fear.

Read Genesis 3:6-10.

> How did Adam and Eve feel about their nakedness after the fall? What did it cause them to do?

Instinctually, Adam and Eve sewed some fig leaves together to hide their nakedness from God. We get this, don't we? We fail; we feel ashamed; we hide. We mess up; we fear being found out; we hide. And around and around this pattern goes.

We all attempt to elude shame in different ways. We hide in unhealthy perfectionism, self-preservation, or self-medication. But the only true antidote to shame is to hide in Jesus Christ—to trust Him with all you are and all you have experienced, knowing He accepts you no matter what.

What are some ways you attempt to hide from shame?

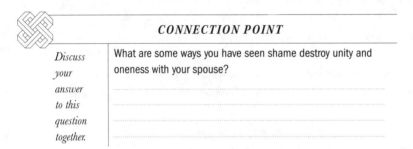

CONNECTION POINT

Discuss your answer to this question together.

What are some ways you have seen shame destroy unity and oneness with your spouse?

It can be painful to consider the things that make us feel shame. Granted, we don't need to dwell in shame, but because of Jesus we don't have to ignore it either. We can lay bare our experiences before Jesus and ask Him to heal our wounds.

Is there a situation of shame you need to lay before God? Write it down and ask Him to help you begin the process of healing by hiding in Jesus.

Christian, you have been covered by the blood of Jesus that has set you free from all shame! But how do we walk in that freedom?

BEING FULLY KNOWN

Have you ever wondered why God used the word *knew* when He was clearly talking about sex? For example: "Now Adam knew Eve his wife, and she conceived and bore Cain . . ." (Gen. 4:1a). Was God too shy to use the actual word? Or was God conveying something else?

The Hebrew word for *knew* is the word *yada*. *Yada* is the active form of knowing and being known in a "variety of senses, figuratively, literally euphemistically, and inferentially." It describes the experience of being seen (physically seeing) and being understood (emotionally perceiving).[4]

We all want to be seen and known—fully, completely, transparently. But we also know that revealing ourselves to another person demands an unbelievable amount of trust and vulnerability. God designed marriage to be the place where you are most fully seen, known, accepted, and loved—body and soul.

CONNECTION POINT

Discuss your answer to this question together.

What is your greatest fear in being fully known by your spouse? If God is bringing to mind something you've been hiding from your spouse, set time aside to share this with him/her. Give the gift of trust as you share.

Fear causes us to flee the presence of God. One way to defeat the lies of fear and shame is by running to the presence of God. Make it a priority this week for you and your spouse to spend time in the presence of God together.

FOR PLEASURE

The world has painted God as prudish, pleasure-hating, stoic, and outdated. Yet it was God who created our bodies with a nervous system that connects seemingly disconnected body parts in pleasure. It was God who designed sex to not only be functional in populating the world, but to also be a wildly exciting experience. It's not God that has a low value of sex—it's us. By taking sex out of the context of marriage, we have minimized its meaning. We will spend more time studying this concept this week, but it is important to understand that one of the purposeful designs of sex was for our enjoyment. God did not create sex and then it accidentally became delightful for people. He intended sex within marriage to be an enjoyable experience.

Read Proverbs 5:18-20.

The last phrase of verse 19 says, "be intoxicated always in her love." Or another way to put it: *Be losing yourself in great pleasure always in her love.*

Is this how you think about sex? Why or why not?

God designed sex to bring great pleasure. What does that teach you about Him?

Some have been taught that sex is purely for the function of having children, or that it is a woman's duty. How does this narrative minimize not only sex, but also how we might view God?

Read 1 Corinthians 7:5.

What is the only activity that should cause married couples to refrain from sex? And for how long should they refrain?

Why did Paul say they should come back together to have sex?

When we submit our bodies and souls to God's good design of sex within the confines of marital covenant, we experience the freedom and joy God intended for this gift.

SEX AS A SACRAMENT

On your wedding day, you made a covenant with your spouse before God, vowing, *I give all of me to all of you.* Every time you have sex with your spouse, it is a physical reminder of the covenant you made on your wedding day. Dr. Timothy Keller said it like this:

> *A* sacrament *is an external visible sign of an invisible reality. That's why it's so meaningful. When you use sex inside of a covenant, it becomes a vehicle for engaging the whole person in an act of self-giving and self-commitment. When I, in marriage, make myself physically naked and vulnerable, it's a sign of what I've done with my whole life. Because by giving up my independence and by making this promise, sex is supposed to be a sign of what you've done with your whole life.*[5]

CONNECTION POINT

Discuss your answers to these questions together.

If you have never considered sex to be this meaningful within your marriage, spend some time processing these questions:

- What has influenced the way I think about sex? Does my belief about sex line up more with how God views sex or with how the world views sex? Or neither? Explain.
- What do you think would change in your sex life if you applied all of these truths we've studied today?
- Do you find yourself checking out during sex? Do you find yourself only giving parts of yourself to your spouse during sex—giving your physical body but not your mind's full attention or your whole heart? Spend some time processing with God what you are holding back from your spouse and ask God to help you engage with your whole person in the sacrament of sex.

God is a good God. And a good God can only create what is good. Sex within marriage is intended to be a good experience! If this has not been the case in your marriage, there is hope. Make a date to talk about your sex life with your spouse. Discuss ways you can prioritize learning and growing in God's good design for sex.

 ## AS YOU GO

Remember this truth: "Therefore a man shall leave his father and his mother and hold fast to his wife, and they shall become one flesh" (Gen. 2:24).

Fight for this truth: God desires for you to know and experience your spouse on every level of body and soul. The freedom Christ purchased for you on the cross is more powerful than any shame Satan tries to stick to you.

Pray this truth: *God, thank You for Your Word. Thank You for teaching me . . .*

Help me to trust and obey You with . . .

Amen

DAY

2

BROKENNESS
TO WHOLENESS

Father,

I believe You want me to be whole—
complete, lacking in nothing. Help me to
surrender every part of my brokenness to
You. Heal me and make me whole. Help me
to trust You to redeem all the ways sin has
deceived me and distorted my view of sex.
Amen

The promise of the gospel is to redeem every part of us,
including our sexual brokenness. Saying "I do" to your
spouse does not magically erase your sexual brokenness,
but saying "I do" to Jesus promises that one day all of your
sexual brokenness will be made whole.

SIN NATURE

We are all sexually broken. Sexual brokenness is not just
about being sexually active before marriage, infidelity
inside of marriage, or looking at porn. These are faulty and
narrow definitions. We are all sexually broken because we
have inherited a sin nature. Dr. Juli Slattery defined sexual
brokenness beyond "the presence of symptoms. *It is anything
that keeps us from experiencing sexuality as the gift and metaphor
of covenant love.*"[6]

> Consider Dr. Slattery's definition of sexual
> brokenness. What are some ways you have not
> experienced sexuality as a gift?

How have your negative experiences shaped the way you view sex today?

SEXUAL IMMORALITY

As we just read, sexual brokenness isn't only about sexual sin. However, sexual brokenness is a human condition that often plays out as sexual immorality. Everything we do with our bodies should honor God. We cannot separate what we do to and with our bodies from what is happening in our hearts or our souls. Jesus spent a good portion of His Sermon on the Mount clarifying the true meaning of the law—the action of our bodies is connected to our spirit's motivation. Attempting to separate one from the other will end in hypocritical asceticism.

Read the following passages: 1 Corinthians 6:18 •
1 Corinthians 10:8 • Ephesians 5:5 • 1 Thessalonians 4:3 •
Hebrews 13:4.

What do all of these verses have in common?

Paul and the writer of Hebrews made it clear our bodies are not meant for sexual immorality. The Greek word for *immorality* is *porneia*, from which we get our word *pornography*.[7] It refers to all illicit sexual activity. Sexual immorality is more than cheating on your spouse, looking at porn, or fantasizing. Sexual immorality is anything you do with your body or mind that lacks sexual integrity. The body is not meant for sexual immorality, but for the Lord, and the Lord for the body.

Read Romans 12:1-2.

Eugene Peterson paraphrased Romans 12:1-2 like this:

> *So here's what I want you to do, God helping you:*
> *Take your everyday, ordinary life—your sleeping,*
> *eating, going-to-work, and walking-around life—and*
> *place it before God as an offering. Embracing what*
> *God does for you is the best thing you can do for him.*
> *Don't become so well-adjusted to your culture that*
> *you fit into it without even thinking. Instead, fix your*
> *attention on God. You'll be changed from the inside*
> *out. Readily recognize what he wants from you, and*
> *quickly respond to it. Unlike the culture around you,*
> *always dragging you down to its level of immaturity,*
> *God brings the best out of you, develops well-formed*
> *maturity in you.*
> **ROMANS 12:1-2, THE MESSAGE**

What did God say your body is for?

Paul warned that we should not be conformed to think the way the world does; rather we should be transformed by the renewal of our minds.

What are some ways you think about sex that have been crafted by the world? What truths do you need to consider to begin renewing your mind to think about sex the way God does?

What are some ways you have given your body over to sexual immorality that you need to repent of?

BROKEN BOUNDARIES

The world sells the lie that God's boundaries for sex are proof that He is irrelevant to the topic. The entire sexual revolution of the 1960s was built on the idea that sexual freedom could only happen if sex had absolutely no constraints or limits. But if we took an honest and sober look at history, the sexual revolution did nothing but breed mass amounts of sexual brokenness. The world says God doesn't value sex. But if God doesn't value sex, why would He spend so much time teaching us how to protect it from being distorted, misused, or misunderstood? God sets boundaries around sex not to keep people from enjoying it, but to show its preciousness, its sacredness, its high value.

Sexual brokenness at the hands of another is heart-wrenching. God cares deeply for you and longs for you to experience healing and wholeness. If you have experienced sexual trauma, we encourage you to seek the counsel of a trusted pastor, leader, or counselor. You can find hope and healing in Christ.

CONNECTION POINT

Discuss your answers to these questions together.

Ignoring or breaking the sexual boundaries God has set breeds sexual brokenness. How have you seen the proof of this statement?

....

....

....

How do you see freedom being replaced with oppression when God's boundaries are broken?

....

....

....

SEXUAL WHOLENESS

Wholeness is the state of being perfectly well in body, soul, and spirit (1 Thess. 5:23). Because our sexuality affects all of who we are, pursuing wholeness in the area of sexuality is a huge part of experiencing wholeness in Christ.

Read Isaiah 61:1-4 (CSB). Isaiah is prophesying about the purpose and ministry of the coming Messiah. Highlight everything Jesus was anointed and sent to do.

> ¹ *The Spirit of the LORD GOD is on me,*
> *because the LORD has anointed me*
> *to bring good news to the poor.*
> *He has sent me to heal the brokenhearted,*
> *to proclaim liberty to the captives*
> *and freedom to the prisoners;*
> ² *to proclaim the year of the LORD's favor,*
> *and the day of our God's vengeance;*
> *to comfort all who mourn,*
> ³ *to provide for those who mourn in Zion;*
> *to give them a crown of beauty instead of ashes,*
> *festive oil instead of mourning,*
> *and splendid clothes instead of despair.*
> *And they will be called righteous trees,*
> *planted by the LORD*
> *to glorify him.*
> ⁴ *They will rebuild the ancient ruins;*
> *they will restore the former devastations;*
> *they will renew the ruined cities,*
> *the devastations of many generations.*

Jesus promises to heal your broken heart and to free you from what enslaves you. As true as this promise is for eternal security, it's true for sexual sin, sexual brokenness, sexual addiction, and sexual trauma. Many of us feel like our sexual brokenness goes too deep for us to ever experience freedom on this side of heaven. But Jesus promises healing.

Take a step of faith and write a prayer in response to this promise. From what sexual sin do you want Jesus to set you free? What brokenness do you want Jesus to heal?

In verse 3, Jesus promised three exchanges—
something good for something bad. What did Jesus
say He will provide?

To give them a:

_____ instead of _____

_____ instead of _____

_____ instead of _____

Jesus promises to provide healing, freedom, and
wholeness instead of brokenness, addiction, and shame.
Through Jesus, we are "creative restorers." We are no
longer bound by our brokenness.

Spend a few moments imagining what a healthy,
restored, and whole sex life could look like.

Pray these "instead" prayers for your sex life:
God, change my posture to what I can give my
spouse instead of what I can get from my spouse.

God, help me to be naked and unashamed with my
spouse instead of feeling shame, fear, or insecurity.

Write a few of your own prayers that are specific to
your marriage. What are some areas you want to
seek wholeness instead of brokenness?

*The ESV Study Bible
commentary on
Isaiah 61 says this
prophecy is about "The
return from Babylonian
exile, but more than
that: spiritual freedom
from the oppression
of sin and Satan.
. . . The poor become,
through the Messiah,
creative restorers of
the sad situations
that man has had to
live with for so long
(cf. 54:3; 58:12).
Every human ideal
falls into ruins in this
world of death, but
the new culture of
life in the city of God
will thrive forever."* [8]

Read 1 Peter 2:24.

Jesus' body was broken to heal our brokenness. Jesus bore our sins to pay our penalty. Jesus endured the wounds of rejection, shame, and betrayal so that we might experience freedom through the healing work of the gospel.

> *Satan's ultimate agenda isn't simply to distort sexuality. He wants to sabotage the gospel. He's interested not just in keeping us from the truth as a concept but in keeping us from the Truth in the person of Jesus Christ.[9]*
>
> **DR. JULI SLATTERY**

CONNECTION POINT

Discuss your answers to these questions together.

How do you redeem sexual wholeness in your marriage? Dr. Slattery counsels couples to establish these three things in their marriages.[10] Spend time processing how you and your spouse can follow this counsel in your marriage.

1. **Make sexual wholeness a priority in your marriage.** Are there experiences you have not yet processed with your spouse that affect your view of sex? Do you need to confess sexual sin to your spouse? Do you have unmet expectations about sex that have caused you to dislike sex?

2. **Fight counterfeit intimacy as a team.** We cannot fight for sexual wholeness alone. We need the body of Christ to help us surrender our brokenness to the Healer. What barriers keep you from inviting your spouse to help you fight sexual sin? Who is a trusted man (for the husband) and trusted woman (for the wife) you could invite to help you fight for sexual wholeness?

CONNECTION POINT

Discuss your answers to these questions together.

3. ***Invite God into your sexual intimacy.*** Prayer changes everything. Consider the "imagination exercise" you did on page 167. Write a list of ways you would like to see God enhance and heal your sex life.

....

....

AS YOU GO

Remember this truth: "The Spirit of the LORD GOD is on me, because the LORD has anointed me to bring good news to the poor. He has sent me to heal the brokenhearted, to proclaim liberty to the captives and freedom to the prisoners" (Isa. 61:1, CSB).

Fight for this truth: No part of you is broken beyond repair. Jesus' body was broken to fully save and heal you once and for all.

Pray this truth: *God, thank You for Your Word. Thank You for teaching me . . .*

Help me to trust and obey You with . . .

Amen

AWAKEN LOVE

Father,
Awaken me—body and soul—to experience the intoxicating love and pleasure that You created sex to be. Transform our sex life—from dissatisfying to satisfying, from good to great, from painful to pleasurable, from a place of brokenness to a place of wholeness. Awaken desire and delight.
Amen

The Old Testament book Song of Solomon (called Song of Songs in some versions) is a scandalous and provocative read. It's full of descriptions of intoxicating desires, steamy sex scenes, and uninhibited discovery of body and soul. In fact, it's so erotic that Jewish doctors advised young people from reading it until they were thirty.[11] (Thirty!!!) The Christian church has followed suit by making it a rarely read or taught text.

Paul said, "All Scripture is breathed out by God and profitable for teaching, for reproof, for correction, and for training in righteousness, that the man of God may be complete, equipped for every good work" (2 Tim. 3:16-17). All Scripture—including the poetry about married love—is given to us for the purpose of being equipped, knowledgeable, and empowered to live as God intends for us to live. Song of Solomon teaches about the exquisiteness of giving your entire body and soul to another in the bonds of commitment. It shows us that the overwhelming sexual desires we feel are given to us by God and are not something to be ashamed of while also teaching us that our desires do not rule us.

Discuss your thoughts on this book together.

If you have never read Song of Solomon straight through, set aside twelve minutes this week to read it from beginning to end. If possible, read it aloud with your spouse. Try not to get too hung up on the poetic images that feel foreign. Rather, ask God to help you see the intent of the poetry.

WHOM MY SOUL LOVES . . .

Let's talk about intimacy for a moment. How would you define *intimacy*?

Shana Schutte said,

> *Being intimate involves the mixing of our life with another's, a mingling of souls, a sharing of hearts. This is something we all long for because it's how God made us. We were designed to connect. . . . Real intimacy makes us feel alive like we've been found, as if someone finally took the time to peer into the depths of our soul and really see us there.*[12]

Sex and intimacy are not synonymous. Should intimacy be a part of your sexual relationship? Absolutely. But intimacy is more than physical touch. Marriage has seasons when, for various reasons, physical intimacy is not possible. But that doesn't mean that deep oneness can't continue to be developed. Our words have the power to creatively restore and awaken love.

Read Song of Solomon 3:1-5.

Notice how many times she said, "whom my soul loves." It seems she was saying that she loved him with her mind, will, and emotions as much as she longed to one day show him that love with her body.

> In the appropriate spaces, write down what you love about your spouse's mind (the way he/she thinks; what he/she thinks about), your spouse's will (the way he/she discerns, makes decisions; how he/she chooses things), and your spouse's emotions (how he/she shows feelings; how he/she processes feelings). Share your thoughts with your spouse.

MIND

WILL

EMOTIONS

In Song of Solomon 4:1-15 the man described the woman. And in 5:10-16 she described him.

> Read the two passages, noting the specificity and detail about what they admire about one another. How can using words of detail and specificity awaken love in a marriage?

CONNECTION POINT

*Discuss
your poem
together.*

Think about your spouse—from head to toe—and write your own
poem of desire in the space below. Make a plan for each of you
to share your poem of desire with one another.

We can use our words to creatively restore and awaken love in our marriages. We all know how good it feels to be told by our spouses how beautiful we are to them, how much they delight in our friendship and intimacy, and how captivated and intoxicated they are by us. Yet many of us struggle to say those things to our spouses.

What are some of the barriers that keep you from telling your spouse how you feel about him/her?

Spend a few moments asking God to give you the courage and creativity to speak words of love and delight to your spouse.

Just as important as it is to speak words of affection and desire to our spouses, we must be open to receiving their words. We've all been there— our bodies are just not what we want them to be, and we feel insecure. For instance your spouse says to you, "I think you're beautiful. You're flawless." But you refuse to receive the compliment, choosing instead to continue to compare yourself to others or replay the negativity and lies the enemy is whispering in your ear. Insecurity about body image is bound to come up throughout marriage. Choosing to believe your spouse's words is a step of faith toward awakening love.

Write out a prayer asking God to help you believe all the good things your spouse thinks and says about you. Ask God to make you receptive to His truth and the truth of your spouse and deaf to the lies of Satan.

SEXUAL FREEDOM

It might surprise you to know that very few things God says are off-limits within the boundaries of a covenant marriage. Unless God explicitly says no to something, or it is not beneficial to producing sexual wholeness, then go for it!

CONNECTION POINT

Discuss your answers to these questions together.

Spend some time processing the following questions with your spouse:
- What is the best sex we have ever had? What made it good for you?
- I like it when . . .
- Remember that time we . . .
- If you could have sex anywhere, where would it be?

But let's keep in mind the truth found in 1 Corinthians 6:12: "'I have the right to do anything,' you say—but not everything is beneficial. 'I have the right to do anything'—but I will not be mastered by anything" (NIV). We have sexual freedom in marriage, but not everything is beneficial.

> *Nothing is supposed to master us. In other words, nothing is more important than God and what He has called us to. God has called us to love our spouses selflessly. If some act in the marriage bed has become more important than the feelings of our spouses, then we are misaligned. The act has mastered us.*[13]
> **RUTH BUEZIS**

Part of sexual freedom in marriage is being selfless in sex. What are some ways you want to put your spouse's feelings and pleasure above your own?

THE BLESSING OF DIFFERENCES

God created men and women to be different—on purpose. An often-quoted illustration is that a man has one on/off switch and a woman has a complex system of knobs, dials, and buttons that need constant tuning and adjustment.

Why do you think God made men and women's bodies so different?

Read Philippians 2:3-4.

How can our differences serve our calling to be selfless and considerate of others when it comes to sexual intimacy?

God made a husband's body and a wife's body different—not to cause disconnection—but to create a lifetime of intimacy, exploration, and communication. Poet John Keats said, "Touch has a memory."[14] Lore Ferguson Wilbert wrote in *Handle with Care*, ". . . the first time you have sex with your spouse is never as fully satisfying as the one-hundredth or the thousandth. We remember the curves, the spaces, the familiar aches, the pleasures, the small signs of build-up and the crashing of release."[15] Your differences are intended to draw you together in discovery and creativity. Consider this quote by Buezis:

> *Women's complexity creates a lifetime of new understanding, new experiences, and potential. Picture an old stereo component with many knobs and dials. . . . Our husbands get to play with every one of those dials and see what they do. As a husband learns how his wife's body, mind, and soul work, he can dial in sex based on who she is that day. Not just randomly set at the neutral positions, the knobs bring out the best in us for the song that will play. God created us with a million possibilities just waiting to be discovered. We have to embrace our potential, but it takes hard work.[16]*

Wives, your body is not a mistake. God made your body to enjoy sex as much as your husband. You must dispel the lie that God created sex for men and not for women. Husbands, pursue your wife's enjoyment as much as your own. While you cannot make her believe that sex is for her pleasure too, you can help her fight the lie by looking to her interest above your own.

CONNECTION POINT

Discuss your answer to this question together.

What are some ways bodily differences have created barriers to sexual pleasure in your marriage?

Awakening love in marriage is more than sexual intimacy, but it is not less. God made your bodies to respond to one another. When you have sex, your body releases a surge of oxytocin to your brain. Oxytocin, often called the love hormone, is the hormone that impacts our ability to bond.[17] Sex is meant to bond you to your spouse.

When in a disagreement or a season of disconnection or apathy, how could prioritizing sexual intimacy provoke unity?

CONNECTION POINT

Discuss your answer to this question together.

What is one way you can explore the gift of sexual freedom this week?

CREATE SPACE FOR LOVE

It takes time and intentionality to develop romance and deep knowing in a relationship. Between work, kids, pressing obligations, and other stressors, it can feel next to impossible to make your sex life a priority. And it certainly doesn't help that movies sell the narrative that good sex only happens spontaneously. Think about it this way: when you make a plan to do something, you are attributing value to it. Making a plan communicates because you value something so much you are willing to say no to something else to say yes to this. The following is a list of some areas where making a plan will benefit the intimacy of your marriage:

DATE NIGHT

A weekly date night communicates priority and value. Ask your spouse the following questions to make the most out of your date night:

- What is your ideal date night?
- What are some barriers that keep you from enjoying date night (for example: having to set up childcare, make the reservations, etc.)?
- What have been some of your favorite date nights and why?
- If you could go on an extended date night (i.e. romantic vacation), where would you want to go and why?

GIFTS

What we do with our money shows what we value. The gifts don't have to break the bank but putting thought and intention into what you give makes a difference. Even a gift such as being willing to sacrifice time in one area of your life to spend intentional quality time with your spouse communicates and creates value.

- What is your favorite boutique store? Why?
- What type of gift makes you feel most loved? Why?

GROW

We read to learn and grow.

- What would you like for us to read about and grow in together?

COUNSELING

Counselors are gifted to help couples heal, rebuild, and restore. If you find yourself in a stalemate-type of argument or betrayal, seek a biblical counselor for support.

· Is there anything you would like for us to seek counseling on together?

God desires for you and your spouse to have a nurturing and beautiful sex life. But understand that is not just going to happen on its own. It will take communication, sacrifice, and work. Don't neglect this vital part of your godly marriage. Enjoy!

> *Eat, friends, and drink; drink your fill of love.*
> **SONG OF SOLOMON 5:1b, NIV**

AS YOU GO

Remember this truth: "Set me as a seal upon your heart, as a seal upon your arm, for love is strong as death, jealousy is fierce as the grave. Its flashes are flashes of fire, the very flame of the LORD. Many waters cannot quench love, neither can floods drown it" (Song of Sol. 8:6-7a).

Fight for this truth: Awakening love in marriage is more than sexual intimacy, but it is not less. God made sex to be a bonding and physically pleasureable experience between you and your spouse.

Pray for this truth: God, thank You for Your Word. Thank You for teaching me . . .

Help me to trust and obey You with . . .

Amen

TALK
IT OUT

We encourage you to take a few minutes on this day to sit with your spouse and process what you studied this week. Use some or all of the following questions to guide your discussion:

1. Which day of study was your favorite and why?

2. What was the most difficult portion of the study for you and why?

3. Do you feel we are opening ourselves up to be fully known by each other? If so, how is that reflected in our sex life? If not, what can we do to make ourselves more transparent to each other?

4. What can we do to increase the intimacy in our marriage?

5. Do you find it difficult to talk about our sex life? If so, why? What can I do to make it easier for us to communicate in this area of our marriage?

6. How have we let our sexual brokenness hinder our sexual relationship? What do we need to do to be healed and whole in this area?

7. How has this session changed the way you view our sex life?

8. Are you pleased and satisfied with our sexual relationship? If not, what can I do to better meet your needs?

9. Which of the "As You Go" statements really captured your heart? Why?

Finish this day by praying together. No doubt this session has unearthed some things that may be difficult to talk about and work through. Ask God to give you courage, time, and words to communicate and grow to have the sex life He wants you to have.

It's so important that you and your spouse spend quality time together on a consistent basis. You'll need to be purposeful and intentional to make this happen. We want to help. Each week we'll provide one or two simple date night ideas. Of course, "date night" could be a "date morning" or "date afternoon." Whatever best fits your schedule. And if you're wondering what to talk about, feel free to use the designated connection points found throughout this week's study or the discussion questions found on Day 4.

DATE IDEAS FOR THIS WEEK

1. As we said in the session, planning your romantic encounters and times of sexual intimacy doesn't lessen the fun or meaning. In fact, you may find it to be just the opposite. So plan a romantic evening together. Sure, it could be an overnight trip that includes a nice dinner and luxury hotel. However, this date night doesn't have to be expensive. You could find some friends to keep your kids for the night, then cook dinner together, snuggle up for a romantic movie, and enjoy the fun to follow!

2. Prior to the date night, find a few quiet moments together to both answer this: *Apart from our sexual intimacy, I feel the closest to you when we are . . .*

   Make a short list. Use your date night time to do at least one of those things on your list. Keep the list handy and refer to it for other date night ideas.

MISSION

A day is coming in which we will stand before King Jesus. And saints, what a day it will be! More than ever before, we will have eyes to see how much Jesus rescued us from, how magnificent and precious Jesus' blood is, and how momentary our present sufferings and afflictions actually were. We will understand fully what it means to be the beloved of God. And we will eat and drink and be merry—with no tears, no sorrows, and no sin. All will be made new, and we will live in harmony with God for all of eternity.

> *ON THAT DAY— WHEN YOU ARE LOOKING INTO THE EYES OF YOUR SAVIOR, YOUR KING, YOUR HOPE, YOUR EVERYTHING—WHAT DO YOU WANT TO BE ABLE TO SAY ABOUT YOUR LIFE?*

On that day—when you are looking into the eyes of your Savior, your King, your Hope, your Everything—what do you want to be able to say about your life?

God is clear about our purpose here on earth. Everything about our lives—including our marriages—should point people to the glorious grace of the gospel. The clarity of God's design for our lives has made Satan's job clear as well. Satan wants nothing more than to destroy our effectiveness by distracting us from God's call on our lives to love Him above all else and to love our neighbors.

Sadly, the destruction usually doesn't require a spectacular event. All it takes is a small distraction and, more often than not, a small distraction by a really good thing. C. S. Lewis conveyed this truth in Letter XII of

The Screwtape Letters. The chief demon, Uncle Screwtape, wrote to his novice nephew demon, Wormwood, about distracting Christians:

> *You can make him do nothing at all for long periods. You can keep him up late at night, not roistering, but staring at a dead fire in a cold room. All the healthy and out-going activities which we want him to avoid can be inhibited and* nothing *given in return, so that at last he may say, as one of my own patients said on his arrival down here, 'I now see that I spent most of my life in doing* neither *what I ought* nor *what I liked.' The Christians describe the Enemy as one 'without whom Nothing is strong'. And Nothing is very strong: strong enough to steal away a man's best years not in sweet sins but in a dreary flickering of the mind over it knows not what and knows not why. . . . You will say that these are very small sins; and doubtless, like all young tempters, you are anxious to be able to report spectacular wickedness. But do remember, the only thing that matters is the extent to which you separate the man from the Enemy. It does not matter how small the sins are provided that their cumulative effect is to edge the man away from the Light and out into the Nothing. Murder is no better than cards if cards can do the trick. Indeed the safest road to Hell is the gradual one—the gentle slope, soft underfoot, without sudden turnings, without milestones, without signposts.*[1]

None of us want a distracted Christian life. And none of us aim to have a bland marriage that lacks lasting purpose and spiritual fruit. We certainly know you don't! You've proved it by spending so much time and effort diving into the Scriptures and having meaningful conversations with your spouse throughout these weeks. In our last session together, we will finish our study by turning our attention to what Scripture says will bring God the most glory and our marriages the most meaning.

NOTES

REVIEW

1. Which day of study was the most meaningful to you? Why?

2. How does our view of sex affect our expectations about sex?

3. How can shame destroy oneness and unity in a marriage?

4. Why are we so afraid to be fully known, even by our spouses? How can this fear affect our sexual relationships in marriage?

5. How has the world distorted the true meaning of sex?

6. How would you define intimacy? Are sex and intimacy the same thing? Explain.

7. Why is it usually difficult for spouses to discuss sexual issues in their marriage?

8. What are some ways you can create space for sexual intimacy in your marriage?

9. Did you do one of the Date Night ideas? If so, share about your experience. Note: We don't need all the details on this one. ;-)

WATCH THE VIDEO

DISCUSS

1. What part of the video really got your attention? Why?

2. What would you say is the greatest thing about marriage? Why?

3. Do you recognize God's calling in your spouse's life? How can you affirm and encourage him/her in that calling?

4. What does it mean to you to be on mission in your marriage? Explain.

5. What are some of the ways God is using both of you to accomplish His purpose in the world? What are you currently doing to make disciples?

6. Is your marriage a witness to the character of God? Is it showing the heart of God? Is so, how? If not, why not?

7. What could be some of the consequences of not seeing your marriage as being on mission?

8. Part of your mission is pouring into the lives of other couples, especially younger ones. Do you agree with this statement? Why or why not? What are you currently doing to accomplish this part of your mission?

Teaching sessions available for purchase or rent at *LifeWay.com/Complement*

DAY

MARRIAGE ON A MISSION

Father,
I want every breath You give me to matter.
Use every gift, portion of faith, and day
You have given me to point the world
to the hope of Jesus. Show me and my
spouse how You want our oneness to
participate in the flourishing of the world.
Amen

Some of the best marriage advice we received was from an older couple who had been faithful in living lives that made much of Jesus Christ. On the surface their lives looked ordinary. They went to work, went on dates, parented kids, and served at church. But that's where the ordinariness ended. They constantly and consistently invested their lives and marriage in kingdom purposes—especially in discipling younger believers. They generously shared their home, their time, and their wisdom with others.

This was their far-reaching encouragement to us: *Establish your marriage the way you want it to function in five years, ten years, twenty years, and so on.*

We want to pass this counsel on to you. Keep in mind, your marriage isn't primarily about you. You've been brought together to reflect the love of God to the world and make a gospel impact. Since that's the case, we want you to take the time to consider how your marriage can fulfill the Great Commission. Today, we will study the Great Commission and the Great Commandments and consider how to use our marriages to further the kingdom of God.

THE GREAT COMMISSION

A mission is "an important official job that a person or group of people is given to do."[2] Each Christian's mission is defined by the Great Commission.

Read the following Gospel accounts of the Great Commission and fill in the blanks.

Matthew 28:16-20	Go therefore and ▮▮▮▮ ▮▮▮▮ of all nations (v. 19a).
Mark 16:15-20	Go into all the world and ▮▮▮▮ the ▮▮▮▮ to the whole creation (v. 15b).
Luke 24:44-49	. . . repentance for the forgiveness of sins should be ▮▮▮▮ in his name to all nations (v. 47a).
John 20:19-23	As the Father has ▮▮▮▮ me, even so I am ▮▮▮▮ you (v. 21b).

How would you summarize the mission given by Jesus in each of these accounts?

In Matthew's account, Jesus gave a direct command to "make disciples" (v. 19). First, what does it mean to be a disciple? Turn the page and read the commentary from the *ESV Gospel Transformation Study Bible* on the Gospel of Mark to get a good picture of discipleship.

*Discipleship in Mark represents nothing less than
God's ultimate restoration of his universal people to
the original creation-design and purpose—namely,
to "walk with God" (Gen. 5:22-24) and to be restored
as true image-bearers of God (Rom. 8:29; 1 Cor. 15:49;
2 Cor. 3:18; Col. 3:10). . . . Discipleship is not merely
a certain code of conduct for the disciples. Being
a disciple of Christ means joining the people of God
in God's creation, coming under his eternal covenant
and kingly rule, and living in dependence on God
rather than independence from him. We ultimately
see that discipleship in Mark flows from dependence
upon the Master's captivating and exemplary person,
formative teaching, and atoning work.[3]*

Summarize this commentary in your own words.

So how do we go about making disciples? How does Matthew 28:19-20 give us a blueprint for disciple-making? As we go about our lives, we are to lead people to Christ, help them identify with the people of God, and teach them what it means to follow Jesus.

As a married couple, you have to be intentional and deliberate in making the Great Commission a priority for your marriage.

Let's look at three ways you can do that.

1. BE WITNESSES OF GOD'S LOVE.

Read Matthew 22:34-40.

What is the first and greatest commandment?

What is the second?

Why is the order of these two commandments so important,
and what could be the result if we disorder them?

Read 2 Corinthians 8:1-15.

Paul commended the Macedonians for getting the order of
loving God and loving people right. What did Paul say proved
their love was genuine?

The greatest command is to love God with every cell of our being. The
second command, to love others, flows out of the first. Generosity is
evidence that we "get it."

*Read this commentary on how the generosity we show to others
reveals we have received the love of God:*

> *Jesus gave not just a tenth of himself, but all of his
> riches. He embraced poverty so that we might become
> rich (2 Cor. 8:9). His radical act of total self-giving is
> the only thing that can consistently move us to give
> beyond the minimum. In essence, if we don't desire
> to respond to God's grace with sacrificial giving,
> then we have not yet fully understood the nature of
> the gospel. The answer to our motivation problem
> is not adherence to a new command but a more
> thoroughgoing knowledge and experience of the
> extravagant self-giving of Christ.*

If we understand that all we have is a direct result of what Christ has given us, we will be moved to give out of our abundance, to carry others' burdens, and to seek after fairness and equity.[4]

How is generously giving your entire self to your spouse a reflection of the gospel?

Would you describe the love level in your marriage as extravagant and abundant? Why or why not?

Read John 13:34-35.

How did Jesus say people will know you are truly His disciple?

If someone was looking in on your marriage, would your love for one another be a testament that you both are disciples of Christ? If not, what needs to change?

Luke 24:48 says, "You are witnesses of these things." Christian, you are a witness to the transformative power of the love of God.

2. BE PREACHERS OF THE GOSPEL.

Jesus said that in order for us to make disciples of all nations, we must preach the gospel. Preaching the gospel is not reserved for pastors but is commanded to every follower of Christ, male and female, young and old.

What is the gospel? Read the following passages and fill in the blanks.

THE BAD NEWS		THE GOOD NEWS
Romans 3:23 *We have all _____.*	BUT	**Romans 6:23** *The free gift of God is _____ _____ in Christ Jesus our Lord.*
Romans 6:23 *The payment for our sin is _____.*	BUT	**John 3:16** *For God so loved the world that he gave his only Son, that whoever _____ in _____ should not perish but have eternal life.*
2 Thessalonians 1:8-9 *Those who do not obey the gospel will suffer the punishment of _____ _____.*	BUT	**1 John 1:9** *If we confess our sins, he is _____ and _____ to forgive us our sins and to cleanse us from all unrighteousness.*
	BUT **GOD**	**Ephesians 2:4-5** *being rich in _____, because of the great love with which he loved us, even when we were dead in our trespasses, made us _____ together with Christ—by _____ you have been _____.*

In your own words, what is the gospel of Jesus Christ?

We are each called to preach forgiveness of sins, reconciliation by the blood of Jesus, and eternal restoration with our Father. This is the high calling we have as believers, and God can use our marriage to accomplish this great calling.

Read Romans 10:13-15.

Why is it so important for you and your spouse to be preachers of the gospel?

3. SENT INTO THE WORLD.

Jesus said to His disciples, "Go" (Matt. 28:19a). After teaching His disciples about the kingdom of God and showing them that He is the way, the truth, and the life, Jesus told them to go into the world and make disciples. Jesus' entire ministry was based on *transference*. It's the idea that we do not keep what we receive—rather, we give it away.

Jesus loves us, so we love others. Jesus forgives us, so we forgive others. Jesus serves us, so we serve others.

As disciples of Christ called to make disciples of Christ, every part of our lives should center on making disciples. This means that how we love our spouses, how we parent, where we live, what we do with our time, and how we spend our money should all reflect the mission to make disciples.

Read Acts 1:8.

CONNECTION POINT

Discuss your answer to this question together.

Take a few minutes as a couple to define your Jerusalem, Judea, Samaria, and end of the earth. How is God calling you as a couple to be witnesses in those places?

AS YOU GO

Remember this truth: "A new commandment I give to you, that you love one another: just as I have loved you, you also are to love one another. By this all people will know that you are my disciples, if you have love for one another" (John 13:34-35).

Fight for this truth: God has given us the mission to make disciples of all people.

Pray this truth: *God, thank You for Your Word. Thank You for teaching me . . .*

Help me to trust and obey You with . . .

Amen

GOD'S
BELOVED

Father,
You are the One who perseveres us. You
keep us steady; You keep us centered;
You keep us aimed at Your will for our
lives. Would You please persevere my
spouse and me to the very end? May
we be found faithful.
Amen

Before a plane takes off, the flight attendant gives instructions for what to do in case of an emergency. If the oxygen masks fall from the ceiling, put on your oxygen mask first, before trying to help someone else. Why? We cannot help others if we don't have oxygen. The end goal is still to help others, but it requires attending to your own mask first.

The same principle applies in marriage. We are called to bear one another's burdens, pray for one another, encourage one another in the faith, and exhort one another in truth. The reality is that we cannot help our spouse persevere if we are barely persevering ourselves. One of the best ways for us to persevere in the faith is to establish rhythms of spiritual health.

Read Hebrews 3:13.

How can we help other Christians not fall prey to deceit?

Consider this passage in the context of your marriage. What are some ways you have been deceived to believe something contrary to God's purpose for marriage?

The Greek word for *exhort* (*encourage*) is *parakaleō*. It means "to call near, i.e. invite, invoke (by imploration, hortation, or consolation)." Jesus used the same Greek word *parakaleō* in His Sermon on the Mount when He said, "Blessed are those who mourn, for they shall be comforted [*parakaleō*]" (Matt. 5:4).[5] Mourning sin requires seeing sin. Satan's goal is to blind us to our sin by any deceit necessary. When we believe his lies, our hearts are hardened. And a hardened heart does not mourn sin thus missing God's comfort. Let's exhort one another so that we don't fall prey to the deceit of sin.

What does this mean for our marriages? As we focused on earlier in our study, we are called to encourage one another. We are to encourage one another to be ambassadors of Christ, bringing the message of reconciliation to the world around us (2 Cor. 5:20). We are to encourage one another to be disciples of Christ, making disciples who make disciples who make disciples (Matt. 28:17-20). We are to exhort one another to see sin, fight sin, repent of sin, and trust our sin to the work of Jesus. We are to help one another persevere for as long as it is called today.

The greatest exhortation you can give your spouse is to prioritize his/her relationship with Jesus.

Read 1 Timothy 4:6-10.

How did Paul exhort Timothy in his relationship with Christ?

So how often should you exhort your spouse? Simply put: Every. Single. Day. Prioritizing your spouse's spiritual health creates an atmosphere for constant exhortation. But the reality is most of us are running so hard we tend to rely on reactionary care rather than proactive care. Here are a few ways to put proactive care into practice for your own soul and the soul of your spouse: *Prayer, Study, Sabbath, and Supporting Each Other's Calling.*

PRAYER

Constant (1 Thess. 5:17) and consistent (Dan. 6:10) conversation with the Lord is a must for every believer. You should not only pray for your spouse but also with your spouse.

What are some things you need to be praying for your spouse and yourself right now?

Take a moment to pray for yourself and your spouse. And then, the next time you are with your spouse, engage in meaningful prayer for each other together. Moving forward, be intentional about your personal prayer time and your prayer time with your spouse. What do you need to do to prioritize the practice of prayer in your life and marriage?

STUDY

The Bible gives us many reasons to study it—to fight sin (Ps. 119:9-11), to grow in faith (Rom. 10:17), to battle the enemy (Eph. 6:17), and to be spiritually equipped (2 Tim. 3:16-17). Many of us might know, believe, and even value studying the Scriptures, yet it's usually one of the first things that goes when we are busy or distracted.

Read Psalm 1.

How does this passage describe the person who delights in and meditates on God's Word?

God used the imagery of a strong, well-watered, fruit-bearing tree to describe people who are rooted and established in the Word of God. Imagine the redwoods of California—giant trees big enough to drive a car through, with root systems that spread out to one hundred feet and branches that reach to the skies.[6]

If you were to think about yourself as a tree, would you consider yourself a "redwood" of the faith? Why or why not?

What are some barriers that prevent you from spending time studying Scripture?

Spend time with your spouse praying and asking God to increase your appetite for His Word. Also, talk about how you can encourage one another to study God's Word.

SABBATH
Read Isaiah 56:1-2; 58:13-14.

What did God say the results of keeping the Sabbath are?

Read Genesis 2:3.

What did God do on the original Sabbath day?

The command to rest is a simple one. Rest. That's it. Put down your work and remind your heart that God is the One who is actually in control. Like most of God's commands, it is simple to understand but incredibly difficult to do. We find our significance in our work. We enjoy our work. We gain security through our work. It's hard to lay all of these things down even for a moment. Committing to a day of rest is a way to train our hearts to recognize and remember that God knows best what we need.

For some of us, taking a day to rest in God feels impossible.
Write down the reasons (or excuses) you use to justify not
obeying this command.

Because this is a command of God, one of the ways we can exhort our
spouses is by encouraging and helping them establish a weekly rhythm of
rest. This is where it can get a little tricky. Creating space for your spouse to
rest in God will require a level of sacrifice and preparation. It might mean
doing more than your share of housework, taking the kids for a bit, or
giving up some time together.

Circle every activity that helps you feel rested and filled. You
can add in your own activities in the spaces below as well.

reading the Bible	prayer	worship	watching a movie
clean spaces	good food	family	yardwork
being outside	creating	conversation	exercise
time with friends	solitude	napping	parties

CONNECTION POINT

*Discuss
your
answer
to this
prompt
together.*

Write down your ideal way to spend time resting in God.

CONNECTION POINT

Discuss your answers to this exercise together.

God wouldn't need to command us to Sabbath if it wasn't something we struggle to do. For some of us, taking a day to rest in God seems impossible. We find plenty of reasons (or perhaps excuses) to not. So for us to know how to encourage our spouses to fight to Sabbath well and for them to know how to encourage us, we need to know why it's difficult for each of us to take a Sabbath. Begin by checking every reason in the list below that applies to you. We have provided space for you to add more. Then both of you share and discuss your lists together:

- ☐ I don't have time to Sabbath. If I take a day off of work, I'll be so far behind. It's not worth it.
- ☐ I get confused between what is Sabbath and what is self-care. I tend to spend my time doing what I want—and that rarely means spending time with God.
- ☐ I am a stay-at-home parent. My house is my work. How am I supposed to rest when I live where I work?
- ☐
- ☐
- ☐

What are some ways you can support your spouse in having a day of rest? For example: If your spouse struggles to rest in a messy house, make a plan to help get the house ordered and clean the night before his/her Sabbath.

Make a plan together on how you can both enjoy a Sabbath each week. Then write down Scripture that will help combat the lies that say you don't need to Sabbath. Spend some time praying this truth over one another.

SUPPORTING ONE ANOTHER IN CALLING

Oneness in marriage means that husband and wife function as one entity under a common banner of vision and mission. That doesn't mean they don't each have specific ways God is calling them to live out the vision and mission. For instance, Aaron serves as a pastor of our church, and Jamie runs a ministry of writing, speaking, and podcasting. Our jobs are not our mission, but neither do they distract from what we have been called to do and committed our lives to do—preach the gospel of Jesus Christ everywhere we go.

Complement: something that completes or makes perfect; either of two parts or things needed to complete the whole[7]

Let's go back to the garden. God created Adam, then Eve, and they worked together. Each using the different jobs, gifts, talents, strengths, weaknesses, abilities, creativity, and insight that God gave them to cause the world around them to flourish.

Notice this happened before sin entered the world. God created a marriage in which man and woman need one another to make things flourish. Men in marriage cannot do it alone. Women in marriage cannot do it alone.

But then sin did enter the world, and consequences followed. (Review the consequences in Gen. 3:16-19.)

What was first a project that husband and wife worked on together in harmony and compatibility had now been disrupted. Man and woman were meant to complement one another in their work, but sin caused the work relationship to be a breeding ground for distrust, power-grabbing, and insecurity.

While singleness can show the world that Christ is sufficient, marriage can show the world what it looks like for men and women to work together in a way that produces wholeness.

CONNECTION POINT

Discuss your answers to these questions together.

What is one way you can encourage and support your spouse in doing his/her work faithfully before God?

....

....

What are specific personality traits, giftings, and/or abilities that you and your spouse have that complement one another?

....

How do you see God using the combination of your personalities, giftings, and/or abilities to be a unique voice in the kingdom of God?

....

AS YOU GO

Remember this truth: "But exhort one another every day, as long as it is called 'today,' that none of you may be hardened by the deceitfulness of sin. For we have come to share in Christ, if indeed we hold our original confidence firm to the end" (Heb. 3:13-14).

Fight for this truth: We are called to pursue the mission of God for our family as one flesh. To do so, we must make sacrifices and prioritize our personal and marital spiritual health.

Pray for this truth: *God, thank You for Your Word. Thank You for teaching me . . .*

Help me to trust and obey You with . . .

Amen

DAY

3

MARRIAGE MANIFESTO

Father,
We want our marriage to be a beautiful light reflecting Your love for us in a dark world. Show us how to be intentional with our marriage. May You receive all the glory. Amen

A manifesto is simply a declaration of intentions. We want to declare that our marriage's intention is to reflect Christ's unbreakable love for His bride.

Today, we want to help you and your spouse create a manifesto for your marriage. Trying to figure out what is a yes and what is a no for your family can feel stressful. Habakkuk 2:2b says, "Write the vision; make it plain on tablets, so he may run who reads it." Our hope and prayer is that as you and your spouse work through these questions and texts, you will have more clarity about God's mission for your marriage. This will enable you to run well and fight hard for your marriage to the glory of God.

Everything in your marriage must be measured primarily by this question: *Will this decision, action, or attitude reflect a clear and accurate picture of Christ's unbreakable and unending love for His bride?*

Let's look at three simple purposes we are called to as believers in a healthy marriage. 1) Love God. 2) Love spouse. 3) Love others.

1. LOVE GOD.

We love God and aim to have undivided hearts in our worship of Him.

Read the following passages and take a few moments to examine your heart: Exodus 20:3; Psalm 81:9; and Isaiah 42:8.

What does it mean to have no other gods before God?

Examining and assessing our hearts to identify "gods" that have taken the throne of our lives is a lifetime process. Dr. Timothy Keller described the idols or gods of our hearts like this: "An idol is something that we look to for things that only God can give."[8]

What things do you find yourself looking to for the true satisfaction, joy, and meaning that only God can give?

On the next page, Dr. Keller provided four categories of idolatry that help diagnose what our hearts care most about.[9]

POWER (success, influence, winning)	APPROVAL (love, affirmation, relationships)	COMFORT (freedom, privacy, lack of stress)	CONTROL (discipline, self-confidence, assurance)
If you seek power, your greatest nightmare is humiliation.	If you seek approval, your greatest nightmare is rejection.	If you seek comfort, your greatest nightmare is stress or demands.	If you seek control, your greatest nightmare is uncertainty.
People around you often feel used.	People around you often feel smothered.	People around you often feel neglected.	People around you often feel condemned.
Your problem emotion is anger.	Your problem emotion is cowardice.	Your problem emotion is boredom.	Your problem emotion is worry.
My life only has meaning if I have power and influence over others.	My life only has meaning if I am loved and respected by _____ .	My life only has meaning if I have this kind of pleasure experience, a particular quality of life.	My life only has meaning if I am able to get mastery over my life in the area of _____ .

Using the chart, what do you believe is your primary root idol? Why?

What are some ways you've seen yourself worship this idol over God?

What do you imagine a life free from this idol might look like? How would you think, feel, or act more freely?

Diagnosing the things our hearts desire to worship reveals areas of needed repentance and transformation. Moving our hearts toward a singular devotion of Jesus Christ is a lifetime process. We fix our eyes on Jesus, and we surrender our affections to Him over and over and over again.

What changes will you make and what steps will you take to establish a commitment to love and worship God above all else? Be specific.

2. LOVE SPOUSE.

We reflect God's unbreakable love for us through our unbreakable love for one another.

A healthy, vibrant marriage is founded on a covenant of deep oneness. There is no other human relationship on this earth from which we should receive such love, devotion, support, care, intimacy, and delight. A covenant marriage has a unique ministry to the world by showing God's unbreakable love for us through our unbreakable love for one another. The question is and will remain until death do us part—*How can we do better?*

How can you love your spouse more consistently, more passionately, and more singularly than anyone else in your life?

What more can you do to encourage, support, and cheer your spouse on to be and do all that God has called him/her to be and do?

How can you better use the power of your words to establish an environment of affirmation and exhortation?

How can you make intimacy more of a priority in your marriage?

What needs to change so that you consistently see and consider your spouse as more significant than yourself every day?

Choosing to love and honor your spouse is not always easy. Remember, you have the gift of the Holy Spirit to help you choose your spouse over yourself.

Write a prayer asking the Holy Spirit to help you love your spouse with the unbreakable, indomitable, and passionate love that Christ has for His bride.

3. LOVE OTHERS.

We love all image bearers of God and will spend our lives making disciples of all people.

Read Galatians 6:1-10.

What is the main purpose of this passage?

Paul wrote, "Bear one another's burdens, and so fulfill the law of Christ" (v. 2).

How does bearing one another's burdens fulfill the law of Christ?

> *The word* burden *here means, "a weight of personal and eternal significance." It can refer to a character flaw, a struggle, or a moral requirement.*
>
> *We can illustrate the idea of bearing one another's burdens with the picture of a man staggering beneath a heavy load of grain. He must somehow get this grain home to his family, but he is about to crumble beneath its weight. A brother sees his distress and rushes to his aid, lifting a part of the burden and thereby easing the weight of it. Although the supportive one does not assume the whole load, his help allows the struggling one to carry on to his destination.[10]*

It is likely that Simon of Cyrene felt this most acutely when a guard put Jesus' cross on his back (Luke 23:26). Bearing the burdens of others is often romanticized, especially if prompted by the expectation of getting something in return. But the reality is that bearing someone else's burdens requires a level of sacrifice we aren't always willing to give. Nor are we able to bear everyone's burdens. We, as the body of Christ, are meant to bear the burdens together.

The context of Galatians 6:1-10 is how we are to care for each other in the church. We are to help shoulder the load for our brothers and sisters in Christ. However, Paul expanded the boundaries in verse 10.

> What did Paul say in verse 10 that indicates we are to extend our care beyond the church?

Read the story of the good Samaritan in Luke 10:25-37.

> What did the good Samaritan have that the priest and Levite did not (v. 33)?

We all have things that keep us from stopping to help people—we're busy; we're on our way to help someone else; we don't have the resources, and so on. We're not told in this passage why the priest and Levite didn't stop. But what we are told is that the reason the Samaritan stopped was because he had compassion. That compassion was stronger than any reason he might have had to pass the man by.

> Take a few moments to examine your heart. Ask God to help you see, however painful it might be, the real reasons you don't bear the burdens of others that come your way. Repent and receive the grace of the gospel.

Then, process with God: *Whom is my family called to serve? Whom do we know that has burdens we need to help carry?*

What is the first step we need to take to start on this mission?

We want our marriages to matter. We want to leave a legacy behind us. We want to raise up our children to know, love, and honor God with all their hearts. We want our neighbors, coworkers, relatives, friends, and strangers to know Jesus. The reality is that those things aren't just going to happen. Creating and forging a meaningful marriage takes time, effort, and initiative. One step in setting your marriage on this path is by writing a manifesto, a motto, a calling that you are committed to abide by. When big life decisions come up, this statement can help guide you. When suffering, sorrow, or seasons of marital apathy hit, this declaration can get you back on track.

We want to grow marriages that honor God and reflect His love to the world. We want to have marriages where we encourage one another to lay aside the weight and sin that holds us back and exhort one another to run faster, harder, and longer together because, *BECAUSE JESUS.*

MARRIAGE MANIFESTO

As a couple, we have what we call a "Marriage Manifesto." It's just a few simple statements that we want to live by. The manifesto isn't meant to condemn us with how we fail but instead propel us toward what we're meant to be. It's a guide that keeps us centered and focused on who and what is important. And, when things are hard, it points us back to the core of what we've promised each other. Here is our manifesto:

WE WILL LOVE GOD: We will love God, as individuals, with all our heart, mind, and soul. We will center our life on Him. He gets the final word, sets the standard, and gets all the glory.

WE WILL LOVE OUR SPOUSE: Grace and encouragement will be the theme of our relationship. When we are fighting, we choose forgiveness. When we are apathetic, we choose pursuit. When we are hurt, we show up. We are better together.

WE WILL LOVE OTHERS: Our home will be a safe space for all who gather. We commit to welcome, love, embrace, empathize, and listen to everyone, while doing our very best to show them Jesus.

> Now, spend some time together praying, thinking, and discussing your own manifesto. Write it out, declaring what will be your aim. Focus on: 1) How you will love God; 2) how you will love your spouse; and 3) how you will love others.

OUR MARRIAGE MANIFESTO

TALK
IT OUT

We encourage you to take a few minutes on this day to sit with your spouse and process what you studied this week. Use some or all of the following questions to guide your discussion:

1. Which day of study was your favorite and why?

2. What was the most difficult portion of the study for you and why?

3. What does it mean to you for our marriage to be *on mission*?

4. What's our first step in being more intentional in making disciples?

5. Do you see the importance of taking a Sabbath? Explain. What can I do to help make that possible for you each week?

6. In what ways has God uniquely designed us to minister together as a couple?

7. What idols have we allowed to take the place of Jesus in our marriage?

8. Which of the "As You Go" statements really captured your heart? Why?

9. What has been your biggest takeaway from this study?

Finish this day by praying together. Ask God to show you how you can be more on mission as a couple. Talk about all you have learned over these last few weeks and ask God to help you live out the truth.

It's so important that you and your spouse spend quality time together on a consistent basis. You'll need to be purposeful and intentional to make this happen. We want to help. Each week we'll provide one or two simple date night ideas. Of course, "date night" could be a "date morning" or "date afternoon." Whatever best fits your schedule. And if you're wondering what to talk about, feel free to use the designated connection points found throughout this week's study or the discussion questions found on Day 4.

DATE IDEAS FOR THIS WEEK

1. Use this date night to serve together. Choose to work in an ongoing ministry of your church or find a way to serve people in your community. After your ministry time, go out for ice cream or coffee and talk about how you as a couple or as a family can spend more time ministering together.

2. Make this date night a double date night. Invite a younger couple who is married or engaged to join you for dinner, whether out at a restaurant or in your home. Take time to get to know them and let them get to know you. And don't let this be a onetime occasion. Choose to invest your lives and marriage in helping mentor younger couples.

CLOSING / CHALLENGE

#COMPLEMENTSTUDY

Wow. Here we are at the last session of this study. I'm sure you've got marriage all figured out now, right? Of course you don't, and neither do we. This great adventure of marriage that God has set you on will continue to be a learning, shaping, beautiful experience, especially as you live it out in the power and direction of the Holy Spirit. And the twists and turns that come with this journey are part of the joy of this God-designed union He has called you to. Please keep in mind that God is always at work in you, carrying on to completion what He started. Remember that while your marriage can and should be a fun and fulfilling ride for you and your spouse, ultimately you've been brought together to glorify God. As you individually submit your lives to God, He will conform you to the image of His Son, and in so doing, shape your marriage to be a clearer picture of the gospel to the world.

> *DON'T ACCEPT A RELATIONSHIP THAT FALLS SHORT OF THE JOY AND PURPOSE GOD INTENDS FOR YOU.*

So don't settle. Don't be OK with a marriage that just exists. Commit to a marriage that thrives. Don't accept a relationship that falls short of the joy and purpose God intends for you. Grow in Him. Flourish. Move forward in the grace and joy of Christ, loving Him and loving each other, *till death do you part.*

REVIEW

1. Which day of study was the most meaningful to you? Why?

2. Before this study, did you see your marriage as being on mission? Explain.

3. How can you make the Great Commission a priority for your marriage?

4. As a couple, what do you see as your Jerusalem, Judea, Samaria, and end of the earth?

5. What can you and your spouse do to help other couples live on mission?

6. Do you both take a Sabbath? If so, what do you do? If not, why?

7. How can you support your spouse in his/her calling? Why is that so important?

8. Did you create a Marriage Manifesto? If so, would you share it with the group?

9. Did you do one of the Date Night ideas? If so, share about your experience.

WATCH THE VIDEO

DISCUSS

1. What is the most important thing you've learned through this study?

2. What was the most jarring truth you encountered in this study? How did it affect you personally? Your marriage?

3. What pitfalls and pain spots in your marriage were brought to light in this study? How are you addressing those?

4. What other changes have you made or are you planning to make in your marriage because of what you've learned?

5. If you could pass down one word of counsel about how to have a flourishing, godly marriage to an engaged couple, what would it be? And why this word?

6. How do you see the next five years of your marriage being different than the last five years?

Teaching sessions available for purchase or rent at *LifeWay.com/Complement*

GROUP LEADER TIPS

If you are the person or couple designated to lead this study, congratulations! What a blessing to help couples better understand the design and purpose of marriage. Thanks for choosing to lead your group through this study. Below are some important items to think about.

ADMINISTRATION

Here are some questions you'll need to answer as you prepare for and lead the study:

- How can I promote the study?
- Where and what time should we meet?
- How will we purchase and distribute the books?
- How will I contact group members?
- What about child care?
- How will I follow up?

RESPONSIBILITIES

Because of the content and design of the study, your role will be more as a facilitator than teacher. You'll be responsible for setting up and playing the DVD or downloaded video teaching sessions. You'll also drive the review question time and the discussion following the video. If you have a large group of participants, you might consider breaking into smaller groups for the discussion times. If so, you'll need to enlist facilitators for each small group.

TYPICAL SESSION

Please note the agendas listed in the Study Flow section of the How-to-Use guide in the front of your Bible study book. Feel free to adjust and shape the schedule that best fits your group. Also, questions for review and the video discussion prompts will be provided for you on the Group Session pages at the beginning of each session. You have freedom to use all, some, or none of the questions listed, based on your group's need.

GROUND RULES

Because of the content and nature of this study, we encourage you to adopt some ground rules for your group in these areas:

- **Authenticity:** Agree together from the outset that there is no perfect person and no perfect couple. Encourage your group to be honest and vulnerable in its discussion but also keep healthy boundaries about the depth of what each couple shares. The authenticity should not lead to embarrassing, humiliating, or belittling a spouse or anyone else.

- **Confidentiality:** Agree together that what's said in this small group stays in the small group. But be aware that if something is shared in the group or to you personally that is illegal or pertains to abuse, you may have a legal responsibility to report that information to appropriate authorities.

- **Encouragement:** Agree together that the atmosphere of the group and study will be one of encouragement. Agree to cheer each other on and pray for one another, both during the time of the study and after it's completed.

PERSONAL PREPARATION

When it comes to leading your group, please don't wing it. Here are some things you can do to prepare.

- Watch the video prior to the session and choose discussion prompts to use.

- Complete all the personal study for the week and choose review questions to use.

- Pray. Pray for yourself, asking the Holy Spirit to guide you as you lead and have the freedom to work powerfully in your life, marriage, and group. Pray for every member of your group. Don't be surprised if this study surfaces some difficult issues among the couples in your group. Be a prayer warrior for them and intercede on their behalf.

ENDNOTES

Session One

1. David Platt, *Counter Culture: A Compassionate Call to Counter Culture in a World of Poverty, Same-Sex Marriage, Racism, Sex Slavery, Immigration, Abortion, Persecution, Orphans, and Pornography* (Carol Stream, IL: Tyndale, 2015), 138.

2. C. S. Lewis, *The Weight of Glory: And Other Addresses* (New York: Harper Collins, 1949, revised 1980), 26.

3. "Note on Genesis 2:18," *ESV Study Bible*, (Wheaton, IL: Crossway, 2008).

4. Bible Project, "Image of God," March 21, 2016, accessed October 2, 2020, https://bibleproject.com/explore/image-god/#!.

5. Editorial staff, "What does 'Imago Dei' Mean? The Image of God in the Bible, *Christianity.com*, accessed August 17, 2020, https://www.christianity.com/wiki/bible/image-of-god-meaning-imago-dei-in-the-bible.html.

6. Fleming Rutledge, *The Crucifixion: Understanding the Death of Jesus Christ* (Grand Rapids, MI: William B. Eerdmans Publishing Company, 2015), 276.

7. Mark Taylor, "1 Corinthians 13:13," *New American Commentary* (Nashville, TN: Broadman and Holman, 2014), 318, accessed via MyWSB.com.

8. Dr. Timothy Keller, with Kathy Keller, *The Meaning of Marriage: Facing the Complexities of Commitment with the Wisdom of God* (New York: Penguin House, 2011).

Session Two

1. Brennan Manning, *The Furious Longing of God* (Colorado Springs, CO: David C. Cook, 2009), 93–94.

2. Elizabeth Gilbert, *The Signature of All Things* (London: Bloomsbury Publishing Plc, 2013), 415.

3. Matt Slick, "Sanctify, Sanctification," *Carm.org*, accessed August 18, 2020, https://carm.org/dictionary-sanctification.

4. Howard Hendricks, as quoted by Will Mancini, "Epic Quotes on Discipleship from Prof Howard Hendricks," *The Vision Room*, accessed September 4, 2020, https://www.visionroom.com/epic-quotes-on-discipleship-from-prof-howard-hendricks/.

5. *Merriam-Webster*, s.v. "encourage," accessed September 4, 2020, https://www.merriam-webster.com/dictionary/encourage#:~:text=transitive%20verb,warm%20weather%20encourages%20plant%20growth.

6. John Onwuchekwa, *Prayer: How Praying Together Shapes the Church* (Wheaton, IL: Crossway, 2018), 70.

7. Sam Crabtree, *Practicing Affirmation* (Wheaton, IL: Crossway, 2011), 29, 32.

8. *Merriam-Webster*, s.v. "refresh," accessed September 18, 2020, https://www.merriam-webster.com/dictionary/refresh.

9. Dr. Ian Hamilton, "Being An Encourager," *Banner of Truth*, August 15, 2003, accessed September 4, 2020, https://banneroftruth.org/us/resources/articles/2003/being-an-encourager/.

10. *Merriam-Webster*, s.v. "consider," accessed September 4, 2020, https://www.merriam-webster.com/dictionary/consider

Session Three

1. Richard J. Foster, *Celebration of Discipline: The Path to Spiritual Growth* (New York: HarperCollins Publishers Inc., 1978), 111–112.

2. Frank C. Laubach, *Prayer: The Mightiest Force in the World* (Burtyrki Books, 2020).

3. Dr. Russell Moore, "Is Your Marriage Baal Worship?," *Ethics and Religious Liberty Commission of the Southern Baptist Convention*, September 26, 2018, accessed September 8, 2020, https://www.russellmoore.com/2018/09/26/is-your-marriage-baal-worship/.

4. Strong's G5293, *Blue Letter Bible*, accessed September 8, 2020, https://www.blueletterbible.org/lang/lexicon/lexicon.cfm?t=kjv&strongs=g5293.

5. Warren W. Wiersbe, *Be Rich* (Colorado Springs: David C. Cook, 1979, 2012), accessed via MyWSB.com.

6. Drew Conroy, "Tiller's TechGuide: Advanced Training Techniques for Oxen," *Tillers International*, 1995, https://static1.squarespace.com/static/58d68e502994ca9ba729256b/t/5a319a070852298a66dfd059/1513200139191Advanced+Training+Techniques+for+Oxen+TechGuide.pdf.

7. Dr. Moore, "Is Your Marriage Baal Worship?," *Ethics and Religious Liberty Commission of the Southern Baptist Convention*.

8. Vickie Kraft, "Lesson 5: The Truth About Submission" *Bible.org*, January 23, 2007, accessed September 9, 2020, https://bible.org/seriespage/lesson-5-truth-about-submission.

9. Strong's H8669, *Blue Letter Bible*, accessed September 9, 2020, https://www.blueletterbible.org/lang/lexicon/lexicon.cfm?t=kjv&strongs=h8669.

10. Dr. Timothy Keller with Kathy Keller, *The Meaning of Marriage*.

11. Ibid.

12. Scotty Smith, "A Prayer for Trusting God When Trusting Others Is Hard," *The Gospel Coalition*, October 21, 2011, accessed September 9, 2020, https://www.thegospelcoalition.org/blogs/scotty-smith/a-prayer-for-trusting-god-when-trusting-others-is-hard/.

13. Eugene Peterson, *Every Step an Arrival* (Colorado Springs: WaterBrook, 2018), 4.

14. Crossway, "Christ in All of Scripture – John 21:15-19," excerpt from the *ESV Gospel Transformation Study Bible, Crossway*, September 1, 2014, accessed

September 9, 2020, https://www.crossway.org/articles/christ-in-all-of-scripture-john-2115-19/.

15. Strong's G2919, *Blue Letter Bible*, accessed September 9, 2020, https://www.blueletterbible.org/lang/lexicon/lexicon.cfm?t=kjv&strongs=g2919.

Session Four

1. C. S. Lewis, *The Complete C. S. Lewis Signature Classics: Mere Christianity* (New York: HarperOne, 2002), 103.

2. Eugene Peterson, *A Long Obedience in the Same Direction* (Downers Grove, IL: IVP Books, 2000), 23–24.

3. Dr. Tony Evans, "The Emptying of Christ Explained," *Tony Evans: The Urban Alternative*, accessed September 11, 2020, https://tonyevans.org/the-emptying-of-christ-explained/.

4. "Note on Proverbs 17:14," *ESV Study Bible*.

5. Amy Azzarito, "The Most Glamorous Ways to Fix a Broken Ceramic," *Architectural Digest*, June 19, 2017, accessed September 12, 2020, https://www.architecturaldigest.com/story/kintsugi-japanese-art-ceramic-repair.

6. "Reconciliation," *Baker's Evangelical Dictionary of Biblical Theology*, accessed via BibleStudyTools on September 18, 2020, https://www.biblestudytools.com/dictionaries/bakers-evangelical-dictionary/reconciliation.html.

7. Charles Spurgeon, *Commentary on Romans* (Titus Books, 2014).

Session Five

1. Dr. Timothy Keller, "Marriage as Completion: One Flesh," sermon, November 14, 2019, accessed via *PodBean* on September 15, 2020, https://podcast.gospelinlife.com/e/marriage-as-completion-one-flesh/.

2. Dr. Keller, *Meaning of Marriage*.

3. Dr. Shahram Heshmat, "5 Factors That Make You Feel Shame," *Psychology Today*, October 4, 2015, accessed September 16, 2020, https://www.psychologytoday.com/us/blog/science-choice/201510/5-factors-make-you-feel-shame.

4. Strong's H3045, *Blue Letter Bible*, accessed September 16, 2020, https://www.blueletterbible.org/lang/lexicon/lexicon.cfm?t=kjv&strongs=h3045.

5. Dr. Timothy Keller, "Love and Lust," sermon, Redeemer Presbyterian Church, May 6, 2012, accessed via *YouTube* on November 1, 2020, https://www.youtube.com/watch?v=jUWnE6GeOiE.

6. Dr. Juli Slattery, *Rethinking Sexuality: God's Design and Why It Matters* (New York: Multnomah, 2018), 79.

7. "What is the meaning of porneia in the Bible?," *Got Questions*, accessed September 16, 2020, https://www.gotquestions.org/porneia-in-the-Bible.html.

8. "Notes on Isaiah 61," *ESV Study Bible*.

9. Dr. Slattery, *Rethinking Sexuality: God's Design and Why It Matters*.

10. Ibid.

11. Matthew Henry, *An Exposition of the Old and New Testament* (Philadelphia: A. Towar, 1833).

12. Shana Schutte, "What is the Definition of Intimacy? What Does It Mean to be Intimate?," *Focus on the Family*, June 5, 2019, accessed September 17, 2020, https://www.focusonthefamily.com/marriage/what-is-the-definition-of-intimacy-what-does-it-mean-to-be-intimate/.

13. Ruth Buezis, *Awaken Love* (Minneapolis: Awaken-Love LLC, 2018), 129

14. John Keats, *The Poetical Works of John Keats, with a Memoir* (Boston: Little, Brown & Company, 1865), 328.

15. Lore Ferguson Wilbert, *Handle with Care* (Nashville, TN: B&H Publishing Group, 2020).

16. Buezis, 170.

17. Stephanie Pappas, "Oxytocin: Facts About the 'Cuddle Hormone,'" *LiveScience*, June 4, 2015, accessed September 17, 2020, https://www.livescience.com/42198-what-is-oxytocin.html#:~:text=Oxytocin%20is%20a%20hormone%20secreted,snuggle%20up%20or%20bond%20socially.

Session Six

1. C. S. Lewis, *The Screwtape Letters* (New York: HarperCollins, 1942, 59–61.

2. *Oxford Learner's Dictionaries*, s.v. "mission," accessed September 18, 2020, https://www.oxfordlearnersdictionaries.com/us/definition/american_english/mission#:~:text=mission%20an%20important%20official%20job,to%20learn%20more%20about%20it.

3. Hans F. Bayer, "The Gospel in Mark," excerpt from the *ESV Gospel Transformation Study Bible*, via Crossway, April 10, 2019, accessed September 18, 2020, https://www.crossway.org/articles/the-gospel-in-mark/.

4. Note on 2 Corinthians 8:1-15," *Gospel Transformation Study Bible*, (Wheaton, IL: Crossway, 2013, 2018).

5. Strong's G3870, *Blue Letter Bible*, accessed September 20, 2020, https://www.blueletterbible.org/lang/lexicon/lexicon.cfm?t=kjv&strongs=g3870.

6. "About Coast Redwoods," *California Department of Parks and Recreation*, accessed October 30, 2020, https://www.parks.ca.gov/?page_id=22257.

7. *Dictionary.com*, s.v. "complement," accessed September 20, 2020, https://www.dictionary.com/browse/complement?s=t.

8. Dr. Timothy Keller, *Counterfeit Gods* (New York: Penguin Books, 2009), 131.

9. Dr. Keller, *Counterfeit Gods*, 64–65.

10. "What does it mean to bear one another's burdens?," *Got Questions*, accessed September 20, 2020, https://www.gotquestions.org/bear-one-anothers-burdens.html.

Take the Next Step in Your Marriage

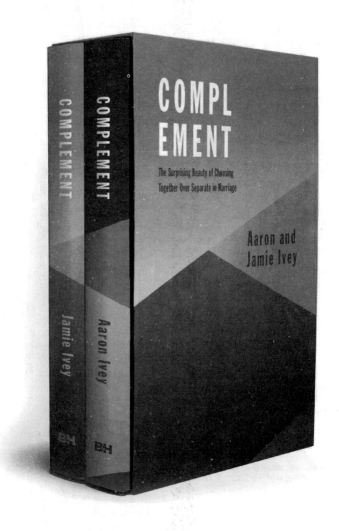